PRYING EYE

PRIVACY IN THE TWENTY-FIRST CENT

For my family
—B.K.

Twenty-First Century Books
A division of Lerner Publishing Group, Inc.
241 First Avenue North
Minneapolis, MN 55401 U.S.A.

Website address: www.lernerbooks.com

Library of Congress Cataloging-in-Publication Data

Kuhn, Betsy.
    Prying eyes : privacy in the twenty-first century / by Betsy Kuhn.
        p. cm.
    Includes bibliographical references and index.
    ISBN 978–0–8225–7179–7 (lib. bdg. : alk. paper)
    1. Privacy, Right of—Juvenile literature. I. Title.
    JC596.K84 2008
    323.44'8—dc22   2007021247

Manufactured in the United States of America
1 2 3 4 5 6 – PA – 13 12 11 10 09 08

TABLE OF CONTENTS

INTRODUCTION   5

PART I // DATA COLLECTION TECHNOLOGIES   18

CHAPTER 1
Say "Cheese": Privacy, Cameras, and Video Surveillance   19

CHAPTER 2
It Had to Be You: DNA and Other Biometrics   31

CHAPTER 3
U R Here: RFID and GPS Technology   51

PART II // DOMAINS OF PRIVATE INFORMATION   64

CHAPTER 4
"At the Schoolhouse Gate": Students and Privacy   65

CHAPTER 5
"Sacred Secrets": Health-Care Privacy   81

CHAPTER 6
Privacy on the Job   91

CHAPTER 7
Data, Data Everywhere: Privacy and Commercial Data   103

PART III //
PRIVACY IN THE TWENTY-FIRST CENTURY   114

CHAPTER 8
Privacy and the War on Terror   115

CONCLUSION
Is Privacy Going, Going, Gone?   131

GLOSSARY   138

SOURCE NOTES   140

SELECTED BIBLIOGRAPHY   148

FURTHER READING AND WEBSITES   149

LANDMARK FEDERAL PRIVACY LEGISLATION   152

LANDMARK U.S. SUPREME COURT CASES
CONCERNING PRIVACY   155

INDEX   157

A person's trash can tell you a lot about him or her. In March 2007, visitors flocked to an exhibit in Paris, France, by two French photojournalists who had collected, sorted, and photographed celebrity rubbish.

INTRODUCTION

To appreciate the ins and outs of privacy, let's talk trash—literally. Consider what people often put in their garbage. They toss in empty prescription bottles, sales receipts, discarded mail, grocery lists, empty ice-cream containers, moldy leftover food, and used Band-Aids. The list goes on and on. Taken together, garbage can reveal some of the most intimate, even embarrassing, details of a person's life. But what do most people do with the garbage on garbage day? They stick it out on the curb!

If the trash is on the curb, is it okay for someone else to come along and go through it?

Two French photojournalists not only pawed through celebrities' garbage, they also mounted it, framed it, and sold it as art. Thanks to Pascal Rostain and Bruno Mouron, thousands of people learned that Halle Berry bought fuzzy toys for her cat. They also found out that someone in Marlon Brando's house drank peach-flavored diet Snapple iced tea.

According to Rostain, garbage reveals "what people eat,

what they are drinking, if they smoke, if they have kids, animals. You can see the personality."

Personally identifiable garbage is even more revealing. For instance, a prescription bottle with a person's name on it or a magazine labeled with a subscriber's name is personal. It is thus more sensitive than an empty can of pork and beans.

Now substitute personal data for garbage. In the course of placing an order online or visiting the doctor, the average person hands over a good deal of personal information. Like garbage, that personal information doesn't just disappear. An online retailer saves every keystroke. A doctor keeps detailed medical records. When a shopper uses a credit card, the credit card company knows what that person bought and when and where the person bought it. What happens to all that information forms the heart of some of the most controversial privacy debates. Who owns all that data? Is there a good reason for maintaining it? Who has access to it?

THE MEANING OF PRIVACY

Privacy can be a fuzzy concept. What one person sees as a violation of privacy might seem unimportant to another. Take the example of garbage again. If asked whether it is okay for someone to snoop in their garbage, most people would probably answer in one of three ways:

1) "I got what I needed out of the stuff I threw away. I don't care what happens to it now."
2) "It makes me kind of uncomfortable, even if there's nothing all that revealing in the trash. But I did put it on the curb, after all."
3) "My garbage is nobody's business but my own. Everyone else should stay out of it!"

Even the wise justices of the U.S. Supreme Court have been unable to really nail down a definition of privacy. There is no clause in the Constitution that specifically guarantees a person's right to privacy. That is one reason the issue keeps coming up. The justices have grappled with it in numerous cases.

"'Privacy' is a broad, abstract and ambiguous concept," wrote Justice Harry Blackmun in 1965 in *Griswold v. Connecticut*. Justice William O. Douglas, in that same case, pointed out that the right to privacy was a "penumbra" of the guarantees of the Bill of Rights. In other words, he thought the right to privacy was implied by the Bill of Rights, but not stated outright. (The Bill of Rights, which includes the first ten amendments of the Constitution, guarantees U.S. citizens certain basic freedoms and rights, such as freedom of speech and religion.)

The most widely accepted explanation of privacy was put forth by Supreme Court justice Louis Brandeis in a 1928 wiretapping case, *Olmstead v. United States*. In this case, which is explained below, the government secretly monitored the telephone calls of a suspect by "tapping" into the telephone wires. It then used information gathered by wiretap to convict him. Justice Brandeis, in a famous opinion in that case, wrote, "The makers of the Constitution undertook to secure conditions favorable to the pursuit of happiness. They conferred, as against the Government, the right to be let alone." That phrase, "the right to be let alone," now stands as one of the classic definitions of privacy. The Fourth Amendment of the Bill of Rights speaks about that right.

THE FOURTH AMENDMENT IN MODERN TIMES

Before the American Revolution (1775–1783), American colonists had no telephones to tap. That hardly meant they

The U.S. Constitution *(left)* was created after the United States gained independence from Great Britain during the American Revolution (1775–1783). The Bill of Rights, approved by all the thirteen states in 1791, included ten amendments (additions) to the Constitution that outlined the basic rights of U.S. citizens.

were free of prying government agents, however. The British government, under King George III, had its own tool for destroying a citizen's privacy. This tool was the writ of assistance. The writ, or written order, was basically a search order used to curb illegal trading. At that time, colonists were forbidden to trade with the French. Many traded with them anyway because doing so was profitable. Using a writ of assistance, a British customs agent could barge into a colonist's home without warning him and search for illegally traded goods. The officers didn't even need to say what they were looking for.

The colonists, naturally, were outraged by this practice. When the framers of the Constitution wrote the Bill of Rights, they wanted to be sure their new government never abused its power in such a way. That is how the Fourth Amendment came to be. It states:

The right of the people to be secure in their persons, houses, papers, and effects, against unreasonable searches and seizures, shall not be violated, and no Warrants shall issue, but upon probable cause, supported by Oath or affirmation, and particularly describing the place to be searched, and the persons or things to be seized.

The Fourth Amendment was the exact opposite of a royal writ of assistance. It guaranteed that if the government wanted to conduct a search, it had to have a written order from a judge to do so. The written order was called a warrant. To obtain it, government agents needed to show the judge a good reason to conduct the search. The agents also had to identify the place they planned to search. Finally, they had to say what it was they were searching for.

The Fourth Amendment provides the strongest constitutional argument for the right to privacy. It was written in 1789, however. There were no telephones, no cell phones, no computers, and no Internet—none of the technologies that are so much a part of modern life. In fact, some of the trickiest Fourth Amendment questions the federal courts have had to address center on how to interpret the amendment in light of new technology. It is one thing to say that a person's house and papers are to be free of unreasonable searches. Does this protection also apply to the person's e-mails?

The practice of wiretapping illustrates how new technology has stirred Fourth Amendment questions. As telephones came into wide use, law enforcement personnel learned how to listen in on suspects' phone calls. They saw wiretapping as an effective means to fight crime. The people whose calls were tapped saw it as a constitutional violation. The wiretap, they said, was a kind of search. Thus, it had to meet the same Fourth Amendment standards as other searches.

A wiretapping case reached the U.S. Supreme Court for the first time in 1928. This was during Prohibition, the years from 1920 to 1933 when a constitutional amendment had made it illegal to sell or manufacture alcoholic beverages. The Bureau of Investigation (BOI, forerunner to the FBI, Federal Bureau of Investigation), which tried to catch people who were violating the law, had its hands full. It was particularly interested in catching bootleggers, people who made or sold liquor illegally. Wiretaps were one of the tools the BOI used in its work.

With a wiretap, BOI agents gathered enough evidence against a bootlegger named Roy Olmstead to convict him of violating the country's Prohibition laws. Olmstead challenged his conviction. He claimed that the use of the wiretap violated his Fourth Amendment right to be free of illegal search and seizure. In 1928 the U.S. Supreme Court decided in *Olmstead v. United States* that the wiretapping evidence did not violate Olmstead's rights. Therefore, the evidence could be used against him in court. The justices' decision was not unanimous. The practice of wiretapping shocked Justice Louis D. Brandeis. He compared it to committing a crime to detect a crime.

"Subtler and more far-reaching means of invading privacy have become available to the Government," he pointed out. "The progress of science in furnishing the Government with means of espionage is not likely to stop with wiretapping. Ways may someday be developed by which the Government, without removing papers from secret drawers, can reproduce them in court, and by which it will be enabled to expose to a jury the most intimate occurrences of the home."

Years later, after many legal twists and turns, the Court decided in 1967 in the case *Katz v. United States* that

This photo, taken in 1966, shows a telephone bugging device used to wiretap telephone conversations.

eavesdropping was a kind of search. Thus, any type of eavesdropping, including wiretapping, required a warrant. In this case, the FBI suspected Charles Katz of illegal gambling. Agents attached an electronic eavesdropping device to the outside of a phone booth from which Katz regularly placed calls. Sure enough, the device recorded evidence of illegal gambling. Katz was convicted. He challenged the conviction, however, on the grounds that the eavesdropping violated his Fourth Amendment rights. The Supreme Court decided that, in using a telephone booth, Katz had an *expectation of privacy*. It didn't matter that he'd placed his call in a glass-sided public booth. "What he sought to exclude when he entered the booth was not the intruding eye—it was the uninvited ear," wrote Justice Potter Stewart. Therefore, his conversation was protected by the Fourth Amendment.

This decision introduced an important distinction in

Fourth Amendment law. Until *Katz*, Fourth Amendment law had focused on a person's rights within his or her home. Now the Fourth Amendment protected a citizen from government intrusion outside the home when the citizen had an expectation of privacy. In other words, the Fourth Amendment protected people, not a place.

Fourth Amendment law underwent more fine-tuning in *Kyllo v. United States*. In 1991 government agents suspected Danny Lee Kyllo, of Florence, Oregon, of growing marijuana in his house under high-intensity lamps. In the wee hours of a January night, the agents scanned Kyllo's home with a thermal imager. This device detects the presence of people or objects from the heat they emit. In this case, the agents used the imager to locate the presence of high-intensity lamps. The agents sat in a vehicle across the street from the building where Kyllo lived, and operated the scanner. It indicated that one portion of the house was much hotter than the rest. Based largely on those results, the agents obtained a warrant to search Kyllo's home. There they discovered that he was, in fact, growing the illegal drug.

Did the use of the thermal imager violate the Fourth Amendment? Kyllo claimed it did. In 2001 the U.S. Supreme Court agreed with him. The government agents, wrote the Court, used "a device that is not in general public use, to explore details of the home that would previously have been unknowable without physical intrusion." In other words, the use of the thermal imager was a type of search, and it required a warrant.

OTHER LAWS THAT PROTECT PRIVACY

The Constitution is just one source of privacy law in the United States, and the Fourth Amendment is its most frequently cited section on issues related to privacy. The Ninth Amendment has played a role in privacy cases too. It states, "The enumeration in the Constitution, of certain rights, shall not be construed to deny or disparage others retained by the people." In other words, just because the founding fathers failed to mention a specific right in the Constitution does not mean the right does not exist. The Fourteenth Amendment has also been used as an argument for the right to privacy. This amendment, among other things, implies that a citizen shall have a right to make personal choices about his or her private life.

Privacy laws also rely on the decisions of state courts and federal and state legislation. To see how these various laws come into play, let's go back to the garbage bin. If a police officer digs through a person's trash and finds evidence of a crime, is that evidence admissible (usable) in court? It would depend on the state in which the crime took place. The Supreme Court has given one answer. State laws sometimes give another.

This question lay at the core of the case *California v. Greenwood*, which the Supreme Court decided in 1988. Jenny Stracner, an investigator with the Laguna Beach, California, police department, suspected that Billy Greenwood was selling narcotics. Stracner asked the trash collector in Greenwood's neighborhood to give her Greenwood's trash, which he did. Repeated inspections of his trash revealed evidence of drug dealing. On that basis, the officer obtained a warrant for a search of Greenwood's home. There inspectors found sizable quantities of narcotics.

Greenwood challenged the search of his garbage without a search warrant. Because the case involved a government agent searching a citizen, the Fourth Amendment was relevant. Eventually, the case reached the U.S. Supreme Court, where the Court ruled against Greenwood. "The Fourth Amendment does not prohibit the warrantless search and seizure of garbage left for collection outside the curtilage of a home," wrote the Court. (Curtilage is the area around a home, such as a yard, where the occupant can reasonably expect privacy.) The Court added, "plastic garbage bags left along a public street are readily accessible to animals, children, scavengers, snoops, and other members of the public."

According to the Supreme Court decision, police should not be expected to operate under a different standard than, say, a hungry dog that smells a bone in a trash bag. A number of states, however, disagreed with the Supreme Court. They held that a police officer should have higher standards than the average mutt. These states have established laws that impose a higher standard than the one set in *Greenwood*. At least six states require a police officer to obtain a warrant before searching a suspect's garbage. In a case decided in 2003 by the New Hampshire Supreme Court, the court held that the contents of "household trash disclose information about the resident that few people would want to be made public. . . . We acknowledge that the United States Supreme Court has held to the contrary. We are free, however, to construe our State Constitution to provide greater protection than the Federal Constitution. We do so here."

Both *California v. Greenwood* and the New Hampshire case pitted a government entity against citizens. Very often, though, it is not a government agent who violates someone's privacy. It is another citizen, a private company, a doctor, or the media.

Imagine that a neighbor is snooping in your garbage. She finds a love letter you wrote but decided against sending. She posts it on the Internet, everyone you know reads it, and you are embarrassed. In this situation, you can't turn to the Constitution. There is no government agent involved. You could instead check state tort laws to see if you have a good case.

A tort is a civil wrong. This type of wrong is committed by one private citizen or group against another private citizen or group. Examples of torts include trespassing and assault and battery. Hence, a person who threatens another with bodily harm can be sued under tort law. Tort law concerning privacy issues is known as *invasion of privacy law*.

Each state has created its own body of tort law in the form of court decisions and statutes. (Statutes are laws enacted by the state legislature.) As a result, tort laws vary from state to state. One state might have strict privacy laws. Another might have almost none.

An invasion of privacy case sometimes touches on a constitutional right even when the government is not involved. Take the example of the love letter. Imagine a newspaper reporter found it and published it in the local weekly newspaper. If you filed an invasion of privacy case against the newspaper, chances are you would lose the case. The court probably would decide that because the First Amendment guarantees freedom of the press, the newspaper had the right to publish the letter.

Despite these laws and regulations, huge holes remain in the nation's privacy laws. There is no comprehensive federal law protecting Internet use, for instance. The lack of a major Internet law reflects a trend in U.S. legal history: new technology tends to be several steps ahead of the law. In addition to the Internet, this is true of emerging technologies such as radio frequency identification (RFID) and biometric (physical trait identification) technology. These two identification tools are becoming increasingly common.

BIG BROTHER

"It was a bright cold day in April, and the clocks were striking thirteen." So began a novel by George Orwell that appeared in 1949. It was called *1984*, and it captured a widespread fear that technology, in the hands of a sinister government, could be used to control citizens.

Winston Smith, the main character, lives in a totalitarian society whose leaders take drastic steps to destroy individuality. "Big Brother Is Watching You," posters remind citizens. Telescreens broadcast a person's every move for the Thought Police.

"Nineteen Eighty-Four is a work of pure horror," said a writer in a 1949 review in the *New York Times*. The book did more than provide gripping reading. It also gave the public the verbal tools to describe their fear that the government would encroach on their private lives. The terms *Big Brother*, *the Thought Police*, and *Orwellian* are still used when the topic of privacy arises.

In fact, there have been times in the nation's history when the government has overstepped its legal boundaries and trespassed on its citizens' privacy. In the 1950s, the United States feared the spread of Communism throughout the world. At the time, the United States was involved in a power struggle with the Soviet Union and other countries with totalitarian, Communist governments. This period of tension was called the Cold War (1945–1991). Fanatical officials were so eager to expose Communists in the United States that they ignored their Fourth Amendment rights.

Later, in the 1970s, President Richard M. Nixon maintained a list of "enemies" who had spoken out against his administration. He illegally used government surveillance to spy on them, and he tried to ruin their careers. When the public learned of these abuses, they were outraged. Their protests brought about some of the most important privacy legislation in the country's history. Under the Privacy Act of 1974 and the revised Freedom of Information Act of that same year, U.S. citizens were given greater access to government records.

AN ABUNDANCE OF DATA

In colonial times, a person's "papers and effects," as the Fourth Amendment puts it, might have included nothing more than a box containing a deed to a house. In modern times, a person's "effects" are scattered in many places: telephone records, financial data, Internet accounts, blood samples, and more. Satellites beam cell phone messages through the skies. Hidden cameras capture people's images. Doctors share their patients' most intimate records with people the patients have never met. With so much data floating around, questions abound about how best to protect it.

The chapters that follow discuss some of the many methods of gathering personal data and their privacy implications. Does a person have the right to photograph a stranger and post the photo on the Internet? Can a principal search a student's backpack? Can the federal government legally tap into the telephone calls of millions of Americans in the name of fighting terrorism? These are just some of the many questions in the modern privacy debate.

This book does not address the issue of privacy as it relates to personal choices such as the right to die, have an abortion, or use contraceptives. These issues bring up areas of law best discussed on their own terms and not mixed in with privacy and personal data.

So read on, and be careful of what you put in the trash!

PART I

DATA COLLECTION TECHNOLOGIES

Camera phones have become increasingly widespread, making it easier for people to capture and distribute digital photos.

CHAPTER 1

SAY "CHEESE": PRIVACY, CAMERAS, AND VIDEO SURVEILLANCE

Cameras are funny things. They can capture an inspiring image, like astronauts walking on the moon for the first time on July 20, 1969. But they can also capture someone's most embarrassing moment. From the time cameras came into general use, photographers have poked their lenses where they were not wanted.

As far back as 1890, legal scholars Samuel D. Warren and Louis D. Brandeis (who later became a U.S. Supreme Court justice) found photographers intrusive. They were so outraged by photographers' insensitivity to their subjects' privacy that they published an article, "The Right to Privacy." This article became a landmark document in privacy law. "Instantaneous photographs and newspaper enterprise have invaded the sacred precincts of private and domestic life," they wrote, "and numerous mechanical devices threaten to make good the prediction that 'what is whispered in the closet shall be proclaimed from the house-tops.'"

In the twenty-first century, cameras seem to be everywhere in a variety of forms, including cell phone cameras, video surveillance cameras, and aerial cameras. All of these cameras can be useful, but they have also introduced new privacy concerns.

YOUR HANDY CAMERA PHONE

Almost every person carrying a new cell phone is equipped to take a photograph or a video. This capability can be valuable. There are many reports of someone snapping a photo of a crime in progress and thus helping the police to make a quick arrest. Hurricane victims have used their camera phones to record the damage to their homes for insurance agents.

There is a downside to the existence of so many tiny cell phone cameras, though. They have made it easy to capture people in embarrassing or incriminating positions. In 2003 Gary Dann was waiting in a store's checkout line. Suddenly, the man in front of him began yelling at the cashier for being unable to process his credit card. Dann took out his phone. Acting as if he were about to place a call, he snapped the snarling man's photo and posted it on his website.

What if the angry man had found out that Dann had taken and posted his picture online? It's unlikely he could have done anything. The incident happened in public. Dann was within his legal right to snap away.

Does that mean that any photograph taken in public is legal? Not necessarily. The question one must ask is, what is a person's expectation of privacy? The angry man at the grocery store had no expectation of privacy. A person changing clothes in a locker room, on the other hand, does have certain privacy expectations.

"The technology is really testing the traditional understanding of the zone of privacy," noted David Sobel of the Electronic Privacy Information Center. "At some point, courts might be inclined to say there are limits to the concept of waiving [giving up] your privacy rights when you're in public."

One legal scholar has even suggested that a new area of tort law might develop to address the area of "public privacy." It would focus on one's privacy expectations while out in public. For instance, cell phones can be used so secretly that it's possible to take photos up a woman's skirt in a public place without her noticing. This practice, known as upskirting, violates the woman's privacy. She may be in a public setting, but she expects that what's under her skirt is private.

States, for the most part, have responded quickly to the potential misuse of cell phone cameras. Most states have laws prohibiting certain kinds of offensive photography. For example, about half of them prohibit upskirting and similar photographs.

Market analysts predict that by 2009, 142 million camera phones will be available for sale. Given such an immense number, it is fortunate that most people use their cell phone cameras appropriately. In fact, privacy experts are more concerned that people will use poor judgment when posting their camera phone photographs online.

"Kids go to these parties, and everybody's going to have a camera," said Nancy Willard, an Internet expert. "They'll post all these really fun pictures on the Internet and maybe post names to go along with the pictures. Nobody has any ability to control what's going to happen with those images." What's more, they can live on in the Internet for a very long time.

THE CITIES HAVE EYES

If a woman strolling down a New York City street had to smile every time she passed a camera, she'd have to smile virtually the entire walk. According to a 1998 study by the New York Civil Liberties Union, volunteers found more than 300 surveillance cameras in an eight-block area. In all of Manhattan, the heart of New York City, they identified 2,397 cameras. Most were operated by private businesses, such as stores and banks. The number of cameras in New York City has increased greatly since then. The terrorist attacks in New York on September 11, 2001, prompted the city to install still more cameras. As these cameras have become more affordable, other cities, from Spokane, Washington, to Easton, Pennsylvania, have considered installing them to help patrol their streets.

Surveillance cameras are legal. A person on a city street has virtually no expectation of privacy. However, there is considerable debate over whether cameras make a city safer. Some reports claim that the cameras have virtually no effect on crime. Criminals, they note, simply move to areas beyond the cameras' scope. Yet, in Chicago, Illinois, police made seventy-six arrests with the help of cameras in just three months in 2006. Even if there were undisputed evidence that cameras reduce crime, the question remains: is the improved security worth the loss of privacy?

In Philadelphia, Pennsylvania, city officials thought surveillance cameras could help curb an increase in armed violence. Before making a decision, they asked the citizens to vote on the video cameras in the May 2006 primary election. A "yes" vote indicated that the voter believed the cameras would be beneficial. The mayor campaigned for the cameras, but other city leaders opposed them. "There's probably no doubt [cameras] will make the city safer," said John O'Connell, leader of the

Surveillance cameras, such as the one at right, are used by businesses and cities and towns in an effort to reduce crime.

Ninth Ward, who opposed the cameras on privacy grounds. "The question is: Is it the best way to make the city safer?"

In 2006, when Fresno, California, began considering the installation of seventy-five cameras, the American Civil Liberties Union (ACLU) of Northern California urged the city to reconsider. "The $1.2 million budgeted for surveillance cameras could be used in much more effective ways such as increased foot patrols, community policing and improved lighting in neighborhoods with high crime rates," said the ACLU's Mark Schlosberg. Besides the fact that the cameras were ineffective at reducing crime, the ACLU noted another problem. They also could "chill speech." In other words, the cameras might discourage innocent people from engaging in legal activities such as demonstrations.

"In London [England] there is a camera for every 13 people and the average person is photographed over 300 times a day," said Schlosberg. "Is this the kind of community we want to live in?" Despite opposition from the ACLU and other groups, Fresno officials decided to move forward with the $1.2 million video surveillance plan. The far smaller city of Bend, Oregon, however, took a different path. They were considering spending $60,000 on a video surveillance system to patrol downtown streets and also pay the salaries of a monitoring staff. Instead, the city assigned a full-time police officer to the area. "For a city our size, that's a more effective way to deal with the security concern," said Andy Jordan, Bend's police chief.

FROM HIGH ABOVE

In 2003 singer Barbra Streisand filed a $10 million lawsuit when an aerial photo of her Malibu, California, estate appeared among 12,700 aerial photos on the California Coastal Records Project website. The photo violated her privacy, she claimed. A Los Angeles Superior Court judge disagreed and found in favor of the website's founder. "Aerial views are a common part of daily living," he said. After all, anyone with an airplane can fly over and photograph a similar image. And airspace over one's home is, by law, part of a "public highway." That is because of a 1946

Barbara Streisand, photographed here at a movie premiere in 2004, felt that her privacy had been violated when the website California Coastal Records Project displayed an aerial photograph of her estate in Malibu, California.

case involving noisy military aircraft and a bunch of dead chickens.

In the case *United States v. Causby*, decided by the U.S. Supreme Court in 1946, a North Carolina chicken farmer complained that noisy military airplanes using a nearby airfield had frightened his chickens to death. He claimed that, due to the noise, 150 of them had killed themselves by flying into walls. The Supreme Court decided against the farmer because the "air is a public highway." The Court added, "Were that not true, every transcontinental flight would subject the operator to countless trespass suits. Common sense revolts at the idea."

Aerial photographs can include street-level views taken by an aerial vehicle. They have become more common, detailed, and accessible. That is why they are the subject of a new high-tech privacy debate.

Pictometry International is a software company that provides searchable, highly detailed photographs of every outdoor square inch of well over one hundred counties. One of its clients is the city of Baltimore, Maryland. Using Pictometry's photographs, city officials can view every building, yard, and inch of sidewalk in their jurisdiction (the area in which they excercise legal power). They can access these photos with the click of a mouse. The photographs will be updated every two years. With this technology, city officials hoped to make it easier for firefighters, police, and rescue personnel to respond to emergencies. They also wanted to streamline the home appraisal process, which assesses homes' values for the purposes of collecting taxes. The city's building inspectors wanted to easily determine whether home and business owners had the proper permits for new construction. Less than a year after adopting Pictometry's system, city housing officials had identified 460 homeowners who had built decks without a permit.

Pictometry has produced detailed aerial images for most large cities in the United States and more than 140 counties. The total area is home to 30 percent of the nation's population.

"On a regular basis, Pictometry helps us get an ambulance to a person who needs help," says Ginger Rudiger, manager of a 9-1-1 dispatch center in rural central Florida. "It's like a magical photo album at your fingertips."

Some privacy experts are concerned about the photographs, and the massive amount of private data they provide. The data shifts the balance of power too much in favor of the government. Yet, said Stacy Mink of the American Civil Liberties Union of Maryland, "One could say there's a legitimate use [of Pictometry's photographs]," particularly since they are not "real-time" photos, such as a surveillance video. The photos were shot once and then downloaded by Pictometry's clients.

This sort of information isn't available only to local governments, however. Microsoft is testing a program that sells Pictometry's images of individual homes for three dollars each. A number of Internet sites, including Google, now offer detailed satellite photos from an ever-growing number of cities and regions. Google notes that the images can be used to check out a potential beach house or a house in the suburbs. The images can be used as a sort of "you are there," real-life map.

The use of satellite photography raises legitimate privacy concerns. Should anyone with an Internet connection be able to zero in on someone's backyard via the World Wide Web? In the wrong hands, an aerial image could show a criminal the best way to enter a home. And isn't there something creepy about having your backyard on the Web for anyone to see?

UNMANNED AERIAL VEHICLES

Real-time aerial photography poses a new set of privacy concerns. The technology used in unmanned aerial vehicles (UAVs) could make real-time aerial images a reality.

There are many different kinds of UAVs. Some are no bigger than a large kite, while others are as big as a full-sized airplane. Although their capabilities differ, they all deliver real-time aerial images to a computer on land. In war zones such as Iraq and Afghanistan, the U.S. military uses UAVs to gather intelligence from high over enemy territory. The 11-foot-long (3-meter) *Shadow 200*, for instance, travels on average 1 mile (1.6 kilometer) above the ground and can record color video. "You get a really good picture," said Staff Sergeant Marvin O. Ward. "You can see people moving around from a long way away."

Until recently, UAVs were used primarily in combat zones. But they are going domestic. The government uses them to

A U.S. soldier prepares the *Shadow 200*, an unmanned aerial vehicle, for launch in Iraq. The *Shadow 200* will fly over designated territory and take photos that will be sent back to a computer for analysis.

Micro air vehicles (MAVs), like this one *(left)*, are light enough to be carried on a soldier's back. These unmanned vehicles can be used as spy planes in war zones.

patrol the U.S.–Mexico border over Arizona. The manufacturers of these vehicles assure the government that they can help patrol ports, pipelines, and more.

Even local governments are hopping on the UAV bandwagon. The Gaston, North Carolina, police department bought a UAV called a Cyberbug in 2006. The department plans to use the Cyberbug to find missing persons, conduct surveillance, take aerial photographs of crime scenes, and combat drug trafficking in open areas. The Cyberbug, which looks like a cross between an immense insect and a tiny airplane, is available in various sizes with wingspans from 15 to 60 inches (38 to 152 centimeters).

There are many questions hanging in the balance, though. What happens if, during a surveillance flight to monitor traffic,

A robotic fly being designed by a team of scientists in California may one day go on spy missions. In one version, Robofly is smaller than a quarter and weighs less than a paperclip. A solar panel supplies energy to a tiny motor, which flaps and rotates the wings 150 times per second, the speed of an actual fly. It can carry a microchip on which it can store photographs or sound recordings.

a UAV reveals criminal evidence that could normally be obtained only with a warrant? Would the evidence be admissible in court? Could UAVs eventually be used by a commercial business to produce real-time aerial photographs for purchase by the general public? Or would the public say, "Not over *my* backyard"?

An employee of a New Jersey school district uses the Iris Access system to enter an elementary school.

CHAPTER 2

IT HAD TO BE YOU:
DNA AND OTHER BIOMETRICS

Biometrics is the science of identifying individuals through their unique physical and behavioral characteristics. Fingerprints, voice patterns, and the patterns of the eye's iris (the colored ring around the eye's pupil) are all used for biometric identification. Behavioral-based methods of identification include analyzing such things as signatures and the way a person walks. All of these biometrics yield one piece of information: a person's identity.

There is another, very different kind of biometric identifier, however: DNA (deoxyribonucleic acid). DNA is the genetic material inside the body's cells that makes each person unique. In each person's DNA lies the genetic code that creates his or her individual characteristics. It determines a person's height, eye color, whether he or she is likely to get certain diseases or high cholesterol, and more. These are details no fingerprint or iris scan could yield. DNA-based biometrics raise the greatest privacy issues. All biometrics have incited at least some controversy, however.

BIOMETRICS GO TO SCHOOL

Gladys Maletzky had been after the UPS deliveryman for weeks. Maletsky was the secretary at Park Avenue Elementary School in Freehold, New Jersey. She was the person who had to let him into the school building every time he made a delivery. He would ring the doorbell, and she'd buzz him in.

Finally, he agreed to do things the new way. Maletzky took a photograph of him and then told him to stare into a scanner. The scanner captured the unique pattern of his iris and saved the information on a database. When he needed to enter the building, he would do what the staff, teachers, and many parents did. He would stop at the aluminum box outside the entrance and have his iris scanned. The doors would unlock automatically as a female voice cooed, "Identification is complete."

Welcome to the world of biometrics, the most effective means of human identification available. In the post 9/11 world, many law enforcement and safety officials have embraced advanced biometric technology as a way of maintaining security. In fact, Park Avenue Elementary School installed its system with the help of a $370,000 grant from the U.S. Department of Justice. As more places use biometric technology, however, concerns about its impact on privacy have grown.

The Park Avenue Elementary School's system illustrates the technology's benefits and disadvantages. On the plus side, the system makes the school more secure against intruders. It also can prevent a divorced parent who has been denied custody of the children from entering the building. On the other hand,

Students wait in line as lunch monitor Joanna Francis has her iris scanned in order to unlock the school doors. In 2003 the system at this school in New Egypt, New Jersey, was used to identify school employees and people authorized to pick up children, but not to identify students.

Freehold isn't a crime-infested community. As one of the school secretaries admitted, the security system is perhaps "a little overkill for a small town." Furthermore, the system does not merely identify an individual. Each person's iris scan is also linked to information in the database, which includes the person's driver's license number. This sensitive piece of data can be used for identity theft. Identity theft is the illegal use of an individual's personal information by another person without the individual's consent or knowledge. By assuming the person's identity, the thief can rob the person in a variety of ways. He or she can withdraw money from the victim's bank account, for example, or get a credit card in the victim's name.

Parents of Park Avenue students can choose whether or not to participate in the biometric entry system. Three months into the program, only three hundred of fifteen hundred parents had undergone a scan. Of those who chose not to participate, many declined for reasons of privacy.

Lillie Coney, of the Electronic Privacy Information Center, agreed their concerns are valid. "Eventually [the data] is going to be used in ways that have nothing to do with" school, she said. If the government decided it needed to access the information, it probably could do so as a result of the new security laws passed after 9/11. Note, however, that these concerns focus on the data stored with the biometric identifier (the iris scan). They do not focus on the identifier itself.

Iris scans in a school setting are rare. Many school cafeterias, however, use another form of biometric technology. In these cafeterias, students use a fingerprint identification system to pay for lunch. To pay, a student places his thumb or index finger on a finger pad. The pad identifies the student and deducts the cost of the lunch from a prepaid account. Like the iris scanner, this technology has both its supporters and its detractors.

Supporters point out the new system's advantages over the old ones. The old systems usually required students to pay for lunch using a meal ticket or personal identification number (PIN). "[Fingerprint identification] takes three or four seconds," said Sue Holger of La Crescent High School cafeteria in Minnesota. "And we know for sure that Mom's money is going to the right kid."

Students cannot lose their finger the way they can a meal card or ticket. They also cannot forget their finger the way they can a PIN number. Accounts are set up so that parents can make deposits online, see exactly what foods their children bought, and block food purchases such as ice cream bars. The system also maintains information on students' food allergies.

Thus, it can alert a student who's buying a menu item that will trigger an allergic reaction. It saves teachers the time it would take them to collect lunch money, and it thwarts bullies who go after other kids' lunch money.

What's more, schools with finger-pad systems report that a higher number of students eligible for free or reduced price lunches are buying meals in the cafeteria. Under the old systems, it was often easy for other children to identify the eligible students, who come from families with low incomes. Out of embarrassment, many eligible students chose not to get a cafeteria lunch. When Litchfield Middle School, in Ohio, installed the finger-pad system, the number of students buying reduced-price lunches rose from 63 percent to 73 percent. Other schools report similar results.

A student places his index finger on a fingerprint scanner in the lunchroom of his Akron, Ohio, school.

Detractors worry about the students' privacy. In fact, a small number of students and parents have chosen to opt out of these programs for privacy reasons. Companies that install the systems, such as Food Service Solutions of Altoona, Pennsylvania, stress the steps they've taken to protect privacy. The system, says Mitch Johns, president of Food Service Solutions, does not retain actual fingerprint images. Rather, it retains mathematical formulas based on the fingerprints. The numbers "cannot be reinterpreted into a fingerprint image," he said. "Both parents and students can rest assured that the fingerprint images cannot be used by law enforcement for identification purposes." Thus, if police are looking for a criminal, they can't turn to the school's fingerprint files in the hope of identifying the culprit.

Nonetheless, if a school cafeteria in Michigan installed the system, it would be breaking the law. In December 2000, Michigan's attorney general Jennifer Granholm ruled that the state's school districts could not use "electronic fingerprinting technology to identify a child for school-related purposes." Doing so would violate the state's 1985 Child Identification and Protection Act, which sets forth strict laws concerning the fingerprinting of Michigan children.

For some privacy advocates, the implications of the system are troubling. If young people accept the cafeteria's biometric system, they are more likely to accept a more intrusive system later. "If ever there was a generation that would not oppose a government system for universal ID, it's this one," said Chris Hoofnagle, a privacy expert.

As with iris scans, many opponents do not object to the use of a biometric identifier itself. Rather, they object to the collection of data that is linked to it. A system designed to pay for lunches could expand to maintain additional private information. One company, identiMetrics, offers a system that links the student's fingerprint data with the databases of the school's library, administration, and nurse's office. In other words, what starts as a simple system to pay for shrimp poppers could expand. Eventually it could track information about a student's medications (and therefore medical conditions), attendance, books he or she checks out, and more.

THE BEGINNING OF BIOMETRICS

One of the earliest forms of biometric identification was the Bertillon system, used in the 1800s. The Bertillon system was applied mostly to criminal cases. It used a series of facial and physical measurements to identify an individual. It was not very accurate.

In the 1890s, Sir Francis Galton of Great Britain introduced a

Sir Francis Galton *(left)* studied many fields, including anthropology, geography, meteorology, and statistical analysis. He came up with a way to use fingerprints to identify individuals. His research established the basis for modern fingerprinting to solve crimes.

more reliable method of identification: fingerprints. It wasn't long before police were using fingerprints as a crime-solving tool.

In 1911 Charles Crispi of New York City was accused of breaking into the H. M. Bernstein Brothers factory and stealing three hundred dollars' worth of clothing. He denied his guilt and put forth an alibi. Crispi very well might have been cleared of wrongdoing if not for Lieutenant Joseph Faurot. Faurot, the city's deputy police commissioner, had just returned from a year's stay in Europe. There he had learned about the new identification method of fingerprinting. Visiting the crime scene, he found Crispi's fingerprint on a windowpane. Faced with this evidence, Crispi admitted his guilt and became the first person in the country to be convicted on the basis of fingerprint evidence.

As law enforcement officials began using fingerprints to solve criminal cases, the public began debating the method's implications. "Have your fingerprints been taken?" asked an article in the *New York Times*, dated June 29, 1919. "Perhaps you bridle at the question. Probably you think that none but criminals are listed in the fingerprint indexes." In fact, the article noted, every U.S. soldier and sailor and most bank employees had been fingerprinted. Fingerprinting was useful in cases of lost memory, babies switched at birth, and identifying the dead. It had also spared the falsely accused of being wrongfully penalized.

By 1924 the Division of Identification in the FBI was adding more than two thousand fingerprints a week to its collection under the watchful eye of the bureau's director, J. Edgar Hoover. By 1953 fingerprints were being put to a wide range of uses.

Police used fingerprints to identify "Old Mike," a loner who died in 1953 in an apartment on New York City's Lower East Side. If not for his fingerprints, he would have been buried anonymously in a burial site for the poor.

Fingerprinting was also being used as a controversial weapon during the Cold War. Under a law called the McCarran Act passed during that period, many nonofficial visitors to the United States, including those from the Soviet Union, had to be fingerprinted. The law came under heavy fire, particularly since the Soviets made no such demands on U.S. citizens visiting their country.

Americans, too, were increasingly subjected to fingerprinting in the name of national security during that period. In 1953 David Leff, an American employee of the United Nations who was based in Paris, France, refused to give his fingerprints. He also refused to fill out a questionnaire. It asked, among other things, "Are you now or have you ever been, a member of the Communist Party?" He was ordered to return to the United States and appear before the Senate's Internal Security Committee or face arrest. Leff appealed the order. Eventually, an international court in Geneva, Switzerland, ruled in his favor.

Fingerprinting, in other words, had developed into something quite complicated. Civilian fingerprint records were being used to solve criminal cases. Fingerprints were being used as a tool in national security issues. Could the field of biometric identity get any more complicated?

Yes. And it did, starting the same year as David Leff's ordeal.

In February 1953, scientists Francis Crick, of Great Britain, and James Watson, of the United States, strolled into their favorite pub in Cambridge, England. Crick announced in his bellowing voice that they "had found the secret of life." In fact, in their nearby laboratory, they had discovered the structure of DNA. DNA is that crucial genetic material that makes every person physically different.

One person's DNA is unlike anyone else's (except in the case of identical twins). As a means of identification, a DNA sample is unrivaled. Unlike a fingerprint, it can provide far more information about a person than simply who he or she is. And that's where things get tricky.

DNA: KEEP IT CONFIDENTIAL

Genetic research has made amazing leaps forward since Crick and Watson's discovery in 1953. The international Human Genome Project has completed a rough map of the entire human genetic sequence. It has identified the approximately twenty thousand to twenty-five thousand genes in human DNA. Scientists have developed hundreds of tests that allow people to learn more about their genetic makeup. Hospitals routinely screen newborn babies for certain disorders they may have inherited. If a person suspects that he or she carries the gene for Lou Gehrig's disease, the person can undergo a test to find out for sure. Other genetic tests reveal whether a person is more likely to get certain diseases. For instance, women can be tested for the BRCA-1 gene mutation. If a woman is found to have the mutation, she has a higher-than-average risk of developing breast and ovarian cancer. A positive test result does not guarantee she will develop the disease, however.

The availability of such information brings many benefits. If a test indicates a predisposition, or tendency, to get a disease, a person can make changes to his or her diet or lifestyle. Perhaps the person can take medication to help prevent or delay the onset of the disease. If a test shows that the person faces a crippling or fatal condition, he or she can take steps to help prepare for what's to come. The person might want to plan for the expense of treating the disease, for example.

This information has a potential downside, though. Many people worry that if a DNA test targets them as being at risk for a disease, employers and health insurance companies will use the information against them. What if, for example, a company learns that a new employee has a predisposition to a potentially fatal illness? The new employee shows no symptoms. In fact, he or she might never develop the illness. Can the employer fire that person on the grounds that he or she might get sick, miss days, or even weeks, of work? If the person were to die, the company would need to hire and train a replacement. In addition, an employee with a fatal illness would be likely to have costly medical bills, which could increase the employer's payments for health insurance.

"Genetics tests are rapidly becoming a routine tool for medical diagnosis," reported the Council for Responsible Genetics (CRG). "The information produced by these tests, while potentially valuable for medical treatment, is increasingly used out of context in ways that are contrary to the interests of the patient." A CRG report notes about five hundred cases in which employers and health insurers have used DNA information about a person or a person's family member to drop or deny that person's health insurance or to make an employment decision.

A New England woman was worried about Huntington's disease, which had killed her mother. (Huntington's, a fatal disease that affects the nerves and muscles, has a 50 percent chance of being inherited.) She was concerned that her medical records might prevent her children from getting health insurance. Her solution was to steal from her own medical records. She went to her health clinic and asked to see her records.

"On every other page, 'H.D. risk' was written," she said. "My heart pounded as I read it. Then, I ripped out every page that said 'H.D.' . . . I stole it for my kids' sake so they will be able to get insurance."

Some employers feel they have the right to DNA information for business reasons. In the fall of 2005, for instance, basketball player Eddy Curry was due to sign a new contract worth millions of dollars with the Chicago Bulls. Earlier that year, though, Curry had missed a number of games after suffering an irregular heartbeat. He'd also had chest pains during training camp in 2004. Cardiologists examined Curry and determined that he had a benign arrhythmia. The condition, a slight irregularity in his heartbeat, was not life-threatening.

Before signing Curry to a new contract, the Bulls insisted he take a DNA test to see if he was predisposed to a condition called hypertrophic cardiomyopathy. This disease of the heart muscle is the number-one cause of sudden death among athletes. If Curry tested negative, the Bulls would award him a four-year contract for $32 million. If he tested positive, he would be offered a contract for $400,000 annually. (The positive test would show that he was predisposed to the disease, not that he actually had it.)

Curry refused to take the test. He had already undergone extensive testing by a team of cardiologists. Medical ethicists were interested in this case. They are concerned about moral aspects of medical decisions. The ethicists pointed out that important privacy issues were at stake. Genetic testing, they said, should not be a factor in an employment decision.

What if Curry were to have a heart attack during a game? Would the Bulls be at fault if they didn't take every step medically possible to predict and prevent it? According to Dr. Paul Thompson, who directs the Athlete's Heart Center at Hartford Hospital, in Connecticut, "An athlete with hypertrophic cardiomyopathy should take off his sneakers."

Before being traded to the New York Knicks in 2005, Eddy Curry was asked by his prior NBA team, the Chicago Bulls, to undergo DNA testing to see if he had a potentially dangerous heart condition. The Bulls were going to base Curry's pay and the terms of his contract on the results of the test.

The whole matter became a nonissue when Curry was traded to the New York Knicks. The team did not ask him to undergo DNA testing, but his story brought national attention to the issue of genetic testing. "As far as DNA testing, we're just at the beginning of that universe," said Alan Milstein, Curry's lawyer. "Pretty soon, though, we'll know whether someone is predisposed to cancer, alcoholism, obesity, baldness, and who knows what else. . . . Hand that information to an employer, and imagine the implications." Milstein also pointed out that under the New York laws that govern the National Basketball Association, forcing Curry to take the DNA test would be illegal in that state.

New York is one of more than thirty states that have enacted laws regarding genetic testing and discrimination. At this time, no similar federal law exists to protect all citizens. In April 2007, however, the House of Representatives passed the Genetic Information Nondiscrimination Act (GINA) by a vote of 420 to 3. As of this writing, the Senate has not yet voted on the bill. Representative Judy Biggert, the Illinois Republican who cosponsored the House bill, pointed out that Americans were not taking advantage of the potential benfits of genetic testing.

"And why not?" she asked. "Well, they are concerned that their genetic information will be used by health insurers to deny them coverage and by potential employers to deny them employment. To put it bluntly, we will never unlock the true promise and benefits of sequencing the human genetic code if Americans are too paranoid to get tested."

State legislatures have been more decisive than Congress in creating genetic testing laws. The majority of states have some sort of genetic antidiscrimination law. Although the specifics of these laws vary from state to state, most of them focus on insurance discrimination. Almost every state prohibits health and life insurance companies from using genetic information to assess a person's risk of becoming seriously ill or dying. Alabama law specifically states that insurance companies cannot discriminate based on test results that indicate a person has a genetic predisposition to cancer.

State laws also address employment discrimination. When Wisconsin passed its genetic privacy law in 1991, it became the first to prohibit employers from using genetic information to discriminate against workers. Since then more than thirty state legislatures have enacted laws prohibiting workplace discrimination based on DNA testing.

In 2005 Governor Bill Richardson of New Mexico signed the Genetic Privacy Act. The act goes beyond banning discrimination based on DNA information when hiring or insuring someone. It also bans discrimination when making a decision about whether to offer a loan, credit card, or a mortgage for a home.

Some states go further. Colorado, Louisiana, Florida, and Georgia define a person's genetic information as personal property. Thus, the person controls how and when his or her genetic information is used.

DNA AND THE CRIMINAL JUSTICE SYSTEM

In 1987 Florida officials used DNA evidence to convict a serial rapist. It was the first case in which DNA was used to secure a criminal conviction. By 1989 Virginia law required serious lawbreakers to submit DNA samples for a newly established state DNA database. Soon other states followed Virginia's example. By 2007 every state required anyone convicted of a sex crime or murder to submit a DNA sample. In addition, most states require those convicted of other serious crimes to submit a DNA sample.

In the early days of DNA sampling, an offender generally gave a blood sample for DNA analysis. In the twenty-first century, law enforcement officials usually either take a blood sample or they swab cells from the inside of a person's cheek. A laboratory technician isolates the DNA from the overall sample and takes it through a series of steps to create a DNA profile. The DNA profile is stored on a state database. In addition, state DNA databases are all linked to the Combined DNA Index System (CODIS), run by the FBI. Taken together, these databases now include DNA profiles from about three million people. Law enforcement personnel add profiles on approximately eighty thousand people each month.

DNA evidence has not only helped to convict a slew of criminals but has also established the innocence of wrongly convicted persons. The Innocence Project, based in New York, has been the major force behind overturning these cases. As of May 2006, 180 innocent people had been cleared of criminal wrongdoing based on the results of DNA testing. Many had served years in prison before DNA evidence secured their release.

The success of DNA testing has generated a heated debate, however. At the heart of the debate is this question: if some DNA testing is a good thing, then isn't doing more testing an even better thing? Many people, particularly law enforcement officials, say yes, more is better. Opponents, on the other hand, are working to set limits on DNA testing.

Originally DNA databases included samples from criminals convicted of only the most serious violent crimes. In the early 2000s, many states have taken DNA samples from persons convicted of a wide range of crimes, including nonviolent ones. Some are even misdemeanors, such as shoplifting. Law enforcement officials argue that collecting more samples helps to solve more crimes. For example, Virginia takes DNA samples

Byron Halsey *(second from right)* walks with members of his family and with Barry Scheck *(left)*, codirector of the Innocence Project, upon being freed from jail on May 15, 2007. He had served more than two decades for a crime he didn't commit. DNA testing proved that Halsey had been wrongly convicted of the rape and murder of two little girls.

from all felons who have been convicted of serious crimes. Most of the DNA matches that law enforcement personnel make for violent crimes come from samples taken from criminals who were originally convicted of property offenses, such as burglary.

The most recent trend has been to take DNA from arrestees. They are people who have been arrested for but not convicted of a crime. Louisiana, Minnesota, Texas, and Virginia are among the states that take DNA samples from arrestees. The reasoning behind this approach is that if more DNA samples are available, more crimes will be solved.

Many legal experts, however, contend that taking samples from an arrestee is unconstitutional. "The relevant principle we hold to in the U.S. is innocent until proven guilty," Jim

Harper of the Cato Institute told *USA Today*. The Council for Responsible Genetics spelled out the problem in a recent report. The council noted that in 2009, California plans to take DNA samples from the approximately 425,000 persons arrested annually for felonies. Of these, about 60 percent will probably not be convicted. Yet, innocent or not, their DNA information will be added to state and federal DNA databases.

Opponents also cite a number of practical reasons for restricting DNA sampling to people convicted of serious crimes. The push to collect DNA samples already has created a huge backlog of samples waiting to be analyzed and added to databases. By the end of 2005, California's backlog numbered more than 250,000 samples. Opponents argue that the time it takes a crime lab to analyze DNA from an arrested individual is time better spent on analyzing data from convicted criminals. That is because more than half the time, the arrested man or woman will be found innocent. Meanwhile, one man in California, who was arrested in 2004, had committed thirteen violent crimes in the two years it took his sample to work its way through the backlog.

Furthermore, a bigger DNA database does not necessarily mean a better database. DNA tests can be wrong because of contamination, improper handling of the sample, and misinterpretation. According to the Innocence Project, of seventy-four cases that were wrongly decided because of problems with DNA testing, five samples had been contaminated. Another eleven had been misinterpreted. The more samples that labs are required to test, the greater the likelihood of incorrect results.

Experts point to yet another problem of widening the DNA sample net. Because racial minorities are arrested and convicted in disproportionate numbers to the general population, the resulting DNA database will end up racially skewed. The number of African American men in the DNA database, for instance, will be far out of proportion to the percentage of African American men in the American population.

The solution to that problem, according to some DNA-collection advocates, is to simply establish a national database that would include a DNA sample from everyone.

Privacy experts disagree and so do civil liberties advocates, who are concerned about a person's basic rights. A national DNA database would be impractical, they say. It would overwhelm the already backlogged DNA testing sites, creating more errors. Then there are the privacy implications. Although a DNA sample does not include the full range of a person's DNA makeup, it still includes more personal information than a fingerprint.

Carol Rose of the American Civil Liberties Union commented, "We don't know all the potential uses of DNA, but once the state has your sample and there are not limits on how it can be used, then the potential civil liberty violations are as vast as the uses themselves."

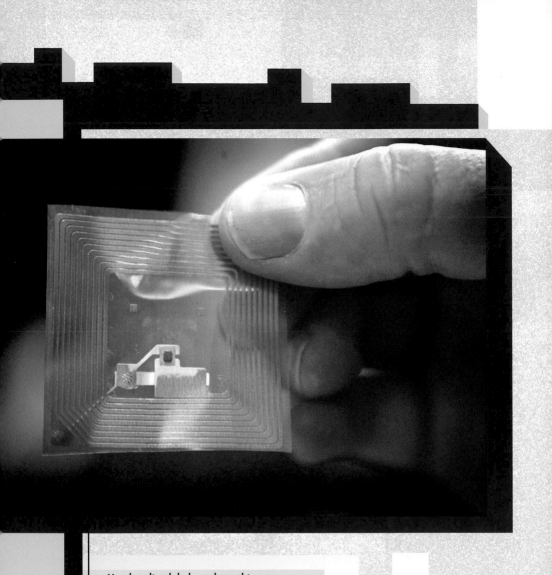

Merchandise labels such as this one use radio frequency identification (RFID) technology to track goods as they travel the globe and into a consumer's hands.

CHAPTER 3

U R Here:
RFID and GPS Technology

In a scene in the movie *Dances with Wolves,* two men traveling through the Old West come upon the skull and bones of someone long dead. One man quips, "Somebody back East is sayin', 'Why don't he write?'"

In the modern world, with its high tech monitoring devices, folks probably wouldn't have to wonder long. Perhaps they could track him by the swipes of his RFID-equipped automatic toll card. Or worried family members could simply trace his location with the GPS (global positioning system) capability on his cell phone.

RFID and GPS devices are becoming increasingly common as tracking devices. They can track a product or person's location. Beyond that, they can also collect vast amounts of data. When used to track people, both technologies have stirred up privacy debates.

CHIPS GALORE

For years, bar-code technology has been the standard for identifying everything from lightbulbs to lemons. A bar code usually appears as a small block of parallel lines in various widths. It holds data that can be read with a scanner, or bar-code reader. The person working at the cash register of a supermarket passes the groceries over the bar-code reader to figure out how much money the customer owes. Recently, however, a new tracking technology called radio frequency identification has burst onto the scene. Because RFID can store far more information than a simple bar code, it has become the tracking system of choice for the military, hospitals, and large retailers such as Wal-Mart. (In fact, Wal-Mart requires its top suppliers to use the technology.) If a military unit in the desert receives a supply drop of fifty identical-looking pallets, soldiers can use an RFID scanner to quickly identify which one contains a needed part for a vehicle.

Bicycle theft was such a problem at Ohio State University, in Columbus, that the school began offering students RFID tags for their bikes. If a bike with an RFID tag is stolen, police can quickly locate it and return it to the student. More than seven hundred students have signed up for the "Bug Your Bike" program. As a result, the school has reported a drop in bicycle thefts.

RFID tags are used to track legal files in large law offices and to find lost pets. One company is even developing a system to help people who raise chickens. Roosters would wear tags to make sure they're mating with hens!

An RFID system consists of an RFID tag, a reader or scanning device, and a database. The tag itself consists of two parts. One is the digital memory chip, which stores information such as a product code and manufacturing information. The second part is an antenna, which can send out radio signals. Beyond those two elements, RFID tags vary. There are passive

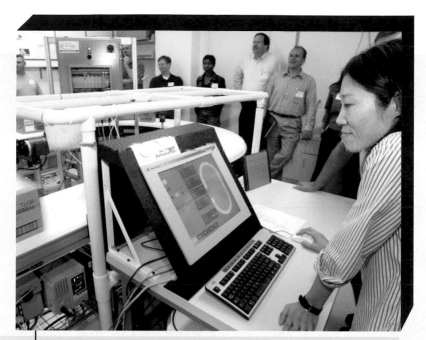

The University of Wisconsin–Madison has dedicated an engineering lab specifically to the study of RFID technology. After graduation, students may be able to help businesses integrate the new technology to keep up with modern retail practices.

tags that send out a signal only in response to a scanning device. There also are active tags that emit a constant signal. Tags can vary in size, the amount of information they can store, the strength and frequency of their signal, and the cost per tag.

A scanning device can be either a handheld implement or a stationary reader (such as a security reader at a store's exit). The device can detect tag signals and send the tag's information to a database. RFID tags can be read through cardboard and fabric. Unlike bar codes, they do not require a direct sight line. This is a straight, unobstructed "view" from the scanner. In addition, while bar codes must be read one at a time, RFID scanners can read multiple tags at once.

RFID technology has become a $2 billion industry. About 1.3 billion tags were sold in 2006. It has been rapidly adopted by businesses and the government with encouraging results. According to one expert, if French emperor Napoleon had had RFID technology, he might have conquered Moscow in the 1812 invasion of Russia instead of running short on supplies! The technological capabilities of RFID and the amount of information the tags can store are considerable. But when used inappropriately, they could create a privacy nightmare, say consumer advocates.

"When the data collected from RFID tags is linked to personally identifiable information, privacy issues can arise," says the Center for Democracy and Technology. Electronic toll cards such as the E-ZPass are a good example. This technology allows drivers to pass more quickly through tollbooths by using a card or a device mounted on the windshield. A scanning device at a toll plaza reads the toll cards as cars drive through. The technology generally allows users to get through the toll plaza more quickly than drivers who pay cash. In return, however, these drivers give up anonymity and personal information. For instance, the toll card company collects data on the date and time each user passes a tollbooth. This information could be used for something other than determining how much the cardholder paid in tolls.

"Almost no one is talking about it publicly, but every day all over the country toll pass information is being used by lawyers in divorce cases," notes Fred Cate, the director of the Center for Applied Cybersecurity Research at Indiana University. The data, for instance, could be used as evidence to prove that a spouse was somewhere other than where he or she claimed to be. In addition, these records show how much time elapsed from when a car passed through one tollbooth to

E-ZPass lanes on a toll road in New Jersey allow drivers who have bought the passes to roll through the tollbooth without having to stop and pay a toll. The E-ZPass system can help alleviate traffic backups by allowing cars to move more quickly through the booth, but it also tracks and stores information about a driver's travel habits.

the time it passed through a second one. Thus, they could be used to nab speeders.

Why, though, is the toll card company saving the data? Once the customer has paid up, is there a legitimate reason to keep it?

Founders of the group CASPIAN (Consumers Against Supermarket Privacy Invasion and Numbering) are so wary of RFID technology that they refer to RFID chips as "spy chips." If chips are placed in individual items, such as underwear, credit cards, shoes, or prescription bottles, they say, it would be easy for people to spy on one another with handheld readers. In 2003 Benetton, the clothing retailer, planned to embed chips in fifteen million individual items of clothing and underwear. CASPIAN responded with an "I'd Rather Go Naked" campaign. The campaign launched an international boycott of

Benetton's goods. As a result, Benetton agreed to hold off on using the implanted chips.

About eight hundred hospitals and ten thousand nursing homes use RFID tags (in the form of bracelets) to track patients, newborns, and elderly residents. The tags are especially helpful for keeping track of those who suffer from memory loss and are prone to wander. The use of RFID to track individuals in these settings has not provoked any opposition so far. However, in other settings, tracking people with RFID has caused quite a stir.

In January 2005, Michelle Tatro's thirteen-year-old daughter came home from school waving a tag on a strap around her neck. "Look at this," said her daughter. "I'm a grocery item. I'm a piece of meat. I'm an orange." It turned out school officials had issued every seventh- and eighth-grade student at her school in Sutter, California, an identification card equipped with an RFID chip. It was a way of simplifying attendance taking. School officials had installed RFID readers in the school's doorways to scan the students' badges as they entered.

Tatro and her husband joined a number of other parents who objected to the badges. They claimed, among other things, that parents had been given no choice about the matter. The badges violated their children's privacy. The students, said Tatro, have "never done anything wrong, and they're being tracked." (While some parents objected to the RFID technology, others objected to the fact that the tags displayed the students' photos and names. They felt the information could endanger children who wore the tags off school grounds.)

"Our children are NOT 'inventory,'" wrote one student's parents. "It is one thing if an employer requires an employee to wear an ID badge as a condition of employment and entirely another to require this of an elementary or junior high student at a public school."

Principal Earnie Graham, who fully supported the new badges, noted, "We've had sixteen cameras on campus for three years and didn't have one complaint when they were put in." The RFID badges were a different story, though. Eventually, as a result of parental objections, the school abandoned them. In fact, state senator Joe Simitian, a Democrat from Palo Alto, California, introduced legislation to prohibit the use of RFID for students for three years. The California legislature passed the bill in 2006, but Governor Arnold Schwarzenegger vetoed (refused to sign) it. Senator Simitian reintroduced the bill in 2007.

"Whatever small gains are to be had from the use of this technology is offset by the troubling message that we send to students when we tag them 'like sheep,'" wrote the bills' authors. The bill's conclusion neatly captures the dilemma concerning RFID technology:

> [B]oth supporters and opponents of this bill generally agree that there are many useful and very promising uses of RFID. Disagreements quickly arise, however, when RFID is used to store personal information or track human movement. . . . Placing RFID tags on pallets destined for Wal-Mart is one thing; forcing our children to wear them is something else entirely. For the parents in Sutter, the few minutes saved by eliminating roll taking was not worth the price. Without recourse to formal legal or policy arguments, one parent at the Sutter school put it aptly and succinctly: "It's creepy."

CHIPS UNDER THE SKIN

"Creepy" or not, the RFID tags in the Sutter, California, school were at least easy to remove. What about an RFID chip implanted under a person's skin? Such chips exist. Although they are tough to extract, a number of people have willingly been "chipped" for the sake of their health, security, or convenience.

A VeriMed microchip, a small tube-shaped RFID about the length of a toothbrush bristle, can be implanted in a patient's arm by injection. This product of the VeriChip Corporation is targeted primarily at people who are likely to require emergency care but may be unconscious during the emergency. These people include diabetics, Alzheimer's patients, and patients with serious heart ailments. Medical personnel, using a VeriChip scanner, can read the patient's verification number from the chip. With this number they can access information on the patient's medical history, the

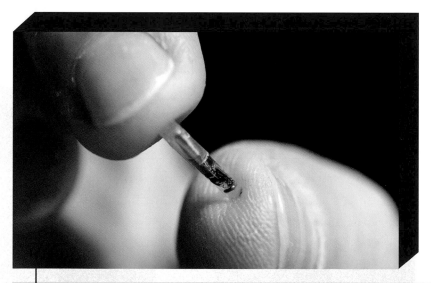

This tiny VeriMed microchip can be implanted into a person's arm and can store important medical and identity information that could potentially help the carrier in a medical emergency. Several futuristic movies and television programs produced in Hollywood have suggested more devious uses for chip implants.

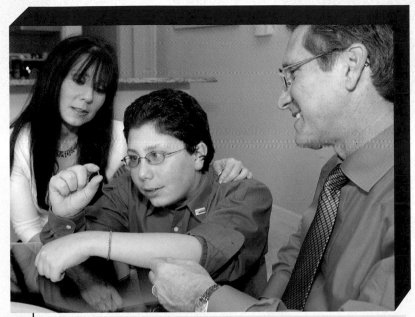

In 2002 Leslie Jacobs *(above left)*, her son Derek *(above center)*, and her husband Jeffrey (not shown) became the first family to receive VeriMed RFID microchip implants. Here they discuss the procedure with Keith Bolton *(right)*, chief technology officer of Applied Digital Solutions, the parent company of VeriChip Corporation.

medications he or she takes, the person's blood type, and any allergies.

As of March 2007, only about three hundred people had had the chip implanted. The company's marketing efforts have included free scanners for hospitals in select cities, but so far business is slow.

Daniel Hickey, a retired naval officer in his late seventies, was one of those who chose to be chipped as a health and safety precaution. Hickey liked the idea that emergency room personnel "can find out everything they need to know right away and treat you better," he said, even if a patient is unconscious. The chip would reduce medical errors and very likely save lives.

As a privacy protection, the device provides only a patient's sixteen-digit identification number. Medical personnel use the number to access the VeriChip database for a person's medical data. Still, privacy experts are skeptical that the information is properly secured and will remain available only to medical personnel.

It can be argued that VeriMed chip's potential to save a person's life is worth the privacy risks. Can the same argument be made about protecting a company's security? The chief executive officer of CityWatcher.com, a video surveillance company, and two of his employees have been implanted with VeriChips. Their chips weren't implanted for medical emergencies. Rather, they grant them access to the company's secured areas, where only some employees may go. A group of staff members at the Justice Ministry in Mexico have also been implanted with chips to speed up their access to similarly secure areas. In other words, these employees are potentially giving up privacy for the security of their company.

What happens when one of these chipped employees takes a new job? They might have new responsibilities, but they will still have the chip. The chips are removable but only with surgery. Hackers, who use their computer skills to access data that is supposed to be secure, are also a danger. A determined hacker could have a ball with RFID chips. At this point, few chips are encrypted. An encrypted chip is written in a special code so that it is unreadable to anyone but rightful users. Even with encryption, technology experts say, most chips are vulnerable to being hacked. Some devices, such as RFID-implanted passkeys (a card that can be swiped in front of a scanner to open a locked door), can be cloned without a good deal of fuss.

Lukas Grunwald, a German security expert, cowrote a program called RFDump, which exposes the security risks of RFID. His program allows him to access and change the data on an RFID chip by using a PDA (personal digital assistant), such as a Blackberry. (The PDA must be equipped with an RFID reader.) His program works regardless of the item tagged with an RFID chip. For instance, he was staying at a hotel that used RFID-equipped key cards. He copied the data from his key card onto his computer. Next, he bought a package of cream cheese, tagged with an RFID price tag, from a supermarket in Germany. Using RFDump, he uploaded the room key card data to the RFID price chip on the cream cheese. "Then," explained Grunwald, "I opened my hotel room with the cream cheese!"

In 2006 staff from *Consumer Reports* magazine conducted a three-month investigation into the RFID industry. A report on their findings concluded that the industry needs to improve security. It noted that consumers, by and large, are "barely aware of" RFID technology, despite the fact that it can be used to collect data about people. RFID tags, said the report, could be read by "any compatible reader within range." The report noted that at least seven states have initiated legislation to protect consumers.

"It's essential to develop the proper framework to protect consumers from the unprecedented privacy and identity theft risks that come with RFID," concluded Andrea Rock, senior editor at the magazine. Despite such concerns, starting in 2006, all newly issued U.S. passports have been equipped with an RFID chip. For security purposes, passports are housed in shielded covers to thwart anyone from reading closed passports. Security expert Bruce Schneier cautions, "Travel abroad and you'll notice how often you have to show your passport: at hotels, banks,

Internet cafes. Anyone intent on harvesting passport data could set up a reader at one of those places."

YOU ARE HERE: GLOBAL POSITIONING SYSTEMS

In the spring of 2006, a Budget rental truck loaded with seven Milton Avery paintings worth millions of dollars failed to arrive at its New York destination. For two weeks, the search for the missing truck yielded nothing. Then someone remembered that a number of Budget trucks had been upgraded with GPS technology. A quick check showed that the missing truck was one of them. In less than an hour, police had found the truck, its contents, and its wayward driver, in Gainesville, Florida.

Satellites that circle Earth are used to collect and transmit all kinds of information. By measuring the distances to the known positions of at least three GPS satellites, a GPS receiver can calculate its location on the surface of Earth to within 6 feet (1.8 m).

The Global Positioning System relies on satellites to send signals that pinpoint a user's location. Originally developed for the U.S. military, GPS has hit the mainstream marketplace. Consumers can buy portable GPS devices for use in cars, on bikes, and on boats. Beginning in December 2005, the federal government mandated that all new cell phones be equipped with GPS technology to improve response time to 9-1-1 emergency calls. Yet, given the GPS capability of identifying someone's location, the technology can be a threat to privacy.

Many parents have embraced GPS technology for keeping tabs on their children, sometimes with the child's knowledge and sometimes without. Teen Arrive Alive allows parents, through GPS technology, to monitor adolescents who drive. For a monthly fee, parents can know exactly where a monitored car is and how fast their son or daughter is driving. With Sprint's Family Locator service, which tracks family members through their cell phones, parents can request that Sprint send them an e-mail if children are not where they said they would be. Apparently, although many parents object to other people monitoring their children through RFID tags and other devices, many of them are comfortable using high-tech devices to track their children themselves.

Yet there are questions about the security of GPS data. "Where you go has to be among the most private and personal things about you," said Lauren Gelman, of the Center for Internet and Society, at Stanford University in California. "You might want to know where your kids are, but do you want the rest of the world to know?"

PART II

DOMAINS OF PRIVATE INFORMATION

A police raid at Stratford High School in South Carolina in 2003 was captured on videotape. Police officers, with guns drawn, forced students to kneel along the wall while drug-sniffing dogs searched for evidence of drugs in students' backpacks.

CHAPTER 4

"AT THE SCHOOLHOUSE GATE": STUDENTS AND PRIVACY

On November 5, 2003, Rodney Goodwin arrived by bus at Stratford High School in Goose Creek, South Carolina. He reported to the cafeteria as usual. Suddenly, Principal George McCrackin appeared. He pointed out Rodney to three policemen. One officer yelled to Rodney and several other students, "Put your hands on the table and don't move! You are under arrest!"

The police officers handcuffed Rodney, who was fifteen years old. They hustled him and the other students into the hallway. There Rodney saw more than one hundred students under lockdown. They lay on the floor, while police officers waved guns at them. A drug-sniffing dog was barking and tearing through the students' backpacks. A police officer pointed a gun at Rodney while Principal McCrackin patted him down and searched his pockets. Another police officer looked through his backpack and shoes.

Rodney didn't know what was going on. "I knew I didn't do anything wrong," he said later. It turned out that Principal McCrackin had heard that a single student had been dealing marijuana. His response was to send in a SWAT (special weapons and tactics) team. The team conducted its search after the majority of the African American students had arrived by bus. (The African American students were less than one-fourth of the student body, but they made up two-thirds of the students targeted in the raid.) The student suspected of drug dealing wasn't in attendance that day. The search uncovered nothing illegal.

The principal's staff, under his direction, captured the whole incident on videotape. Later, a number of students sued the school district for violating their Fourth Amendment

Although Stratford High School's principal, George McCrackin, had called in the police to find suspected drug dealers in the school, the raid turned up no evidence of drugs among the students police targeted.

rights and for use of excessive force. The tape came in handy during the lawsuit.

What happened at Stratford High School is an extreme example. In their quest to keep out drugs and weapons, however, school officials conduct drug tests, search lockers and backpacks, and even bring in drug-sniffing dogs. Students often feel as if their constitutional rights have been swept aside, and a number have filed lawsuits. A few of these cases have been heard in the U.S. Supreme Court. The Court's decisions, which affect millions of students nationwide, have generally sided with the schools. The Court has also imposed some limits on the schools, however.

Access to student records has been another subject of debate. For instance, can a school prevent a student from looking at his or her own records? Can the school share student data with the military? School administrators, students, and parents have not always agreed on the answers to these questions.

THE FOURTH AMENDMENT GOES TO SCHOOL

Until the 1960s, few people thought the rights of students was an important issue. Lawsuits on behalf of students were few and far between. The tide began to turn in the sixties. The civil rights movement had been very effective in establishing new laws extending equal rights to African Americans. It had inspired other groups, such as women, to make their needs heard as well. At the same time, the Vietnam War (1957–1975) was taking more and more American lives. A growing number of people, particularly college students, began to protest the involvement of U.S. troops in the conflict.

Mary Beth Tinker, a thirteen-year-old student in Des Moines, Iowa, thought the war in Vietnam was wrong. On December 16,

1965, she wore a black armband to school in protest, and so did two older classmates. Their political passion failed to impress the principal. He claimed that schools were not a place for demonstrations, and he suspended the three students.

Tinker and the other students filed a lawsuit, challenging the principal's decision. Their case, *Tinker v. Des Moines*, eventually went to the U.S. Supreme Court. In 1969, in a landmark decision, the justices upheld Tinker's right to wear an armband. They also laid the foundation for all future cases involving students' rights.

Students, wrote Justice Abe Fortas, do not "shed their constitutional rights to freedom of speech or expression at the schoolhouse gate."

In *Tinker*, the Supreme Court made it clear that students were not without rights. In the years since, the courts have dealt with a range of cases involving students' rights. Some important cases have focused on student privacy and the Fourth Amendment.

In 1980 a teacher at a Piscataway, New Jersey, high school learned that a student had been smoking in the restroom. She informed the assistant vice principal, who sought out the student. This girl was later identified in court records as T.L.O. When questioned, T.L.O. said that she had never smoked, period. The assistant principal then asked to inspect her purse. Inside, he found cigarettes, marijuana, and written evidence that the girl had been selling the drug.

The assistant principal reported T.L.O. to the police because of the evidence he had found. T.L.O. challenged the search. She said it violated her Fourth Amendment rights to be free of unreasonable search and seizure. The case eventually came before the U.S. Supreme Court in *New Jersey v. T.L.O.*

In a 1985 decision, the Court found that the vice principal

In 1988 U.S. Supreme Court justice Byron White *(left)* wrote the majority opinion in *New Jersey v. T.L.O.* In that case, the Court supported a school official's right to search a student's purse if there were "reasonable grounds" for suspicion.

had acted properly when he searched the student's purse. In a school setting, the Court wrote, a student's privacy interests had to be weighed against "the substantial interest of teachers and administrators in maintaining discipline in the classroom and on school grounds." The Court also maintained that in order to search a student, school officials needed only "reasonable grounds" for doing so. Protecting the school's security could be reasonable grounds for a search. By contrast, police officers in a setting outside of school need to meet the more strict standard of "probable cause" before they can legally conduct a search. Under "probable cause," they must have a good reason to believe a crime has been committed. Given the problems schools faced, like violence and drugs, wrote Justice Byron White, "It is evident that the school setting requires some easing of the restriction to which searches by public authorities are ordinarily subject."

The decision drew fire from many legal experts. It was "extraordinarily spongy," said one lawyer. He thought it invited a distressingly broad range of interpretations. How did one define "reasonable"? Attorney Martin Guggenheim, an expert on juvenile law, put it more bluntly. He said, "What [the decision] really means is that school officials have a license to do as they wish."

In fact, in cases taken up later, the courts have granted school officials even broader search powers. In the case of T.L.O., school administrators were dealing with one student whom they suspected of violating school rules. The problem many school officials face is broader. They suspect drug activity among many students.

DRUG TESTING IS TESTED IN COURT

Such was the case in 1991, in the Vernonia, Oregon, schools. School officials had ample evidence that student drug use was widespread. Student athletes appeared to be in the thick of the drug culture. To fight back, the school tried a new tact—drug testing. Under the program, a student could not participate in sports unless he or she signed a consent form agreeing to undergo random drug testing. Parents, for the most part, supported the new policy.

James Acton, a twelve-year-old student, wanted to try out for the football team. He refused to sign the consent form, however, and the school barred him from the team. His parents, Wayne and Judy Acton, backed their son's decision. In addition, they filed a lawsuit against the school district. They challenged the school's policy on the grounds that it violated the Fourth and Fourteenth Amendment guarantees against unreasonable searches. (A drug test is legally a kind of search.) The Fourteenth Amendment, among other things, guarantees that citizens' constitutional rights cannot be taken away without certain legal procedures.

The U.S. Supreme Court eventually heard the case, *Vernonia School District v. Acton*. In 1995 the Court decided in favor of the school district. Writing for the majority, Justice Antonin Scalia concluded, "Fourth Amendment rights, no less than First and Fourteenth Amendment rights, are different in public schools than elsewhere." School-age years, he wrote, "are the time when the physical, psychological, and addictive effects of drugs are most severe." Therefore, any concerns about privacy and the reasonableness of the tests were easily balanced with concerns about students' safety. In addition, Scalia pointed out, the case dealt exclusively with the testing of athletes. When participating in sports, these students already experienced reduced privacy in locker rooms and showers. A urine test, therefore, had little impact on a student athlete's privacy.

Three justices dissented, meaning they disagreed. Because of the decision in *Vernonia*, wrote Justice Sandra Day O'Connor, the millions of students "who participate in interscholastic sports, an overwhelming majority of whom have given school officials no reason whatsoever to suspect they use drugs at school, are open to an intrusive bodily search." The Court's decision forced students to "prove that they're innocent." The dissenting justices believed testing should have been done only on students suspected of drug use.

Justice Ruth Bader Ginsburg agreed with the majority. She wrote a brief, concurring opinion, in which she pointed out that the *Vernonia* case applied only to student athletes. In other words, the question of whether to test a broader range of students had not been decided yet.

Fast-forward to 1998. That fall, high school student Lindsay Earls signed up for choir and marching band at Tecumseh High

School, in Oklahoma. In the middle of choir class, a teacher asked Earls and some other students to leave class for a drug test. The school had established a new policy because there was evidence of student drug use. Any student in grades seven through twelve who wanted to participate in extracurricular activities could be subjected to random drug tests.

Lindsay Earls did as she was told. She went into the girls' restroom. While teachers stood listening outside the stall, she produced a urine sample.

"It was really awkward," said Earls in an interview with the *Washington Post*. In fact, she found the experience so degrading that she and her parents filed a lawsuit in 1999, challenging the policy. Her father said, "The school has no business interfering with our role as parents and forcing kids to prove their innocence." The U.S. Supreme Court heard the case, *Board of Education of Pattawatomi County v. Earls*, in 2002.

Lindsay Earls *(left)* was photographed in 2001 as a freshman attending Dartmouth College in New Hampshire. In 1999 she challenged her Oklahoma high school's random drug testing policy. Her case went all the way to the U.S. Supreme Court, which decided the policy was constitutional.

The case drew substantial support for both sides. A wide range of groups filed friend-of-the-court briefs, called amicus briefs, on behalf of Lindsay Earls. They included, among others, the American Academy of Pediatrics (AAP). The AAP pointed out that students involved in extracurricular activities were less likely to use drugs and thus made inappropriate targets for tests. "There is a growing recognition that extracurricular involvement plays a role in *protecting* students from substance abuse," the AAP argued in their brief. Drug testing, it noted, was "likely to discourage 'marginal,' higher risk students—whose attachment to school is weakest, but who are in greatest need of protection."

In addition, a group of Oklahoma parents and grandparents filed a brief. They said they opposed "the Policy because it takes parenting away from the parents," and because it "creates an atmosphere of distrust and disrespect at school."

Other organizations put their support squarely behind the Tecumseh school officials. "Eliminating drug use in the American public schools presents one of the greatest challenges of the twenty-first century," noted the National School Boards Association in their amicus brief. "If the schools are to survive and prosper, school administrators must have reasonable means at their disposal to deter conduct which substantially disrupts the school environment." Furthermore, the association noted, the goal of drug testing was not to punish users but to provide them with substance-abuse treatment.

As in *Vernonia*, the high court sided with school officials. "Because this Policy reasonably serves the School District's important interest in detecting and preventing drug use among its students, we hold that it is constitutional," wrote

Justice Clarence Thomas. "A student's privacy interest is limited in a public school environment where the State is responsible for maintaining discipline, health and safety." Because "the school district in this case has presented specific evidence of drug use at Tecumseh schools," the justices found the policy was reasonable.

In *Vernonia*, the court had pointed out that athletes had minimal expectations about privacy because they showered and changed together. Lindsay Earls was not an athlete, though. Her case was relevant for all students who participated in extracurricular activities. How did the decision account for the privacy expectations of, say, members of Future Farmers of America? They probably would not be heading to the showers after a meeting. The Court responded that extracurricular activities "have their own rules and requirements for participating students that do not apply to the student body as a whole." Thus students in extracurricular activities "have a limited expectation of privacy."

This time Justice Ruth Bader Ginsburg dissented. She had noted with foresight in her *Vernonia* opinion that the decision applied to athletes only. Tecumseh High School's policy, wrote Justice Ginsburg, "targets for testing a student population least likely to be at risk for illicit drugs."

The *Vernonia* and *Earls* cases have produced a four-pronged test to determine whether a search of a student (including drug tests) violates the Fourth Amendment. Before conducting a drug test or any other kind of search, the school official must consider the following: (1) the student's expectations of privacy, (2) the type of search to be conducted and its level of intrusiveness, (3) the school's motivation for the search, and (4) how appropriate the response is to the nature of the problem.

The Supreme Court has gradually widened the net to allow

searches of students in a variety of situations. The question is, will schools eventually have the right to search any student for any reason?

The case *Doe v. Little Rock School District* addresses random searches of all students. The student handbook in the Little Rock, Arkansas, school district stated that when "book bags, backpacks, purses and similar containers" were on school property, they could be "subject to random and periodic inspections by school officials." One day in 1999, Little Rock high school employees conducted a random search of all students' belongings. They found marijuana in the backpack of Jane Doe (as she was called in the case). The school reported the finding to the police, and Jane was convicted of a misdemeanor drug offense.

Jane sued the school district on the grounds that the random searches violated the Fourth Amendment. The school maintained that because of the policy in the student handbook, students had a lowered expectation of privacy. They should have expected such a search at any time.

The Eighth Circuit Court of Appeals, which decided this case, said Jane was right and the school was wrong. The school's search did not meet the standards set by the *Earls* case. Specifically, it did not meet the standard regarding a student's expectation of privacy. The fact that the school had set forth its search policy in the student handbook was not a good argument. Students are required by law to attend school, noted the judge. They cannot choose to attend or not attend on the basis of whether they agree with the contents of the student handbook.

The latest trend in student drug testing is checking student athletes for steroids. Some athletes use them to strengthen their muscles and improve their performance, which is illegal. Given the Supreme Court decisions, steroid testing will probably be upheld if it is challenged in court. However, in some states, the state constitution imposes stricter privacy standards than the U.S. Constitution. Students in those states have successfully challenged random searches based on state laws.

Back at Stratford High School, in Goose Creek, South Carolina, parents and students were furious about the way Rodney Goodwin and other students had been treated in 2003. The principal resigned soon after the release of the videotape showing the SWAT teams. As mentioned earlier, some students sued the school district. In July 2006, they settled the case with school officials. As part of the settlement agreement, school officials established a $1.6 million fund to cover the costs of medical and counseling fees for students roughed up in the raid. In addition, under the terms of the agreement, the students of Stratford High School will enjoy the same Fourth Amendment rights that any American enjoys outside of school. The school has no more right to search them than a police officer would. "They are the only students in the nation who have complete protection of their Fourth Amendment rights," said Graham Boyd of the American Civil Liberties Union.

YOUR PERMANENT RECORD

In years past, when a student misbehaved, a principal might very well have peered at him or her in a menacing way and said, "This is going on your permanent record!" The scary part was, the student had no way of knowing whether the principal had carried out the threat. Back then, schools had full control over educational records, and students and parents had virtually no access to them. Yet the school could and did share the records with whomever it chose, including potential employers.

The Watergate scandal in the 1970s changed things. As a

result of that scandal, President Richard Nixon resigned in 1974 after he was linked to a break-in, two years earlier, at the National Democratic Headquarters at Watergate Hotel in Washington, D.C. The men who committed the break-in weren't there to steal staplers. They planned to plant listening devices. As the scandal unfolded, the country learned that Nixon had a history of illegally using government surveillance to gather information on citizens who opposed his presidency and his policies. As a result, Americans began to clamor for more openness from their public institutions, including the office of the school principal. In the process, they learned that school records were very much in need of "sunshine," meaning a policy of openness.

School records were often inaccurate and loaded with personal opinions. For instance, in one document, a teacher described a student as "a real sickie."

U.S. senator James Buckley, a member of the Conservative Party from New York, noted there was "growing evidence of the abuse of student records across the nation." He introduced legislation to address the problem. It was approved by Congress as the Family Educational Rights and Privacy Act (FERPA). President Gerald Ford signed FERPA into law in 1974.

Under FERPA all schools that receive federal funding must offer certain protections for students' educational records. The law applied to private schools as well as public ones, from elementary schools to universities. First, students and their parents have the right to inspect their records and correct or clarify them. Second, FERPA makes it illegal for the school to release certain kinds of information from a student's record without the consent of the student's parents (or, if the student is over the age of eighteen, the consent of the student).

FERPA had its critics. For instance, school and university officials worried about the administrative burden it could create. They also claimed that letters of recommendation, which traditionally were confidential, would lose their meaning. Knowing that the student in question might read the letter, the teachers would submit only the blandest of recommendations, critics feared. Some would argue this prediction has come true.

Since FERPA's passage, Congress has amended the act from time to time. Now a school can share a student's records without the student's or the parents' consent under some circumstances: (1) for certain educational purposes, such as sending the records to another school, where the student plans to enroll, (2) to an organization arranging financial aid for a student, and (3) in response to certain kinds of criminal activity.

THE MILITARY WANTS YOUR NUMBER

The issue of access to student records was raised quietly in Congress in 2002. That year the No Child Left Behind Act was passed in order to improve public school education. The act includes a little-known provision. All secondary middle schools and high schools that receive money from the federal government must provide their students' names, addresses, and telephone numbers to military recruiters. A school that refuses to pass along this contact information will lose its federal funding. Parents can ask the school to take their child's name off a list of contacts the school keeps for the military. However, many parents don't even know that their children's school keeps such a list. Schools do not always do a good job of informing parents.

In 2005 the Portland, Maine, school district gave the military recruiter contact information for 98 percent of its juniors and seniors. When parents realized the situation, they

A U.S. Marine recruiter speaks to a group of seniors at Hoboken High School, in New Jersey. Some school districts are challenging the requirement that schools that receive public funds must provide the military with student contact information.

protested. Portland schools have since revised their policies. Now student information is released only if parents choose to opt *in* to the program. Since implementing the new policy, Portland schools have given military recruiters contact information on just 40 percent of the juniors and seniors.

Other school districts have taken similar steps. Sometimes they have done so under threat of legal action. The Albuquerque, New Mexico, public schools revised their policy after the American Civil Liberties Union of New Mexico threatened them with a lawsuit. Now the Albuquerque schools include a consent form as part of each student's registration packet.

"It's not enough to bury the notice of parents' opt-out rights somewhere on a school website or in a student handbook," said New Mexico attorney Karen Meyer. "The school has to bring the information to parents' attention so they can make an informed and conscious choice."

Thousands of workers in health care and related fields have access to patient medical records. Although the information in these records is supposed to be confidential, there is a risk of it becoming public against a patient's wishes.

CHAPTER 5

"SACRED SECRETS": HEALTH-CARE PRIVACY

Well over two thousand years ago, an ancient Greek was concerned about confidentiality. His name was Hippocrates, and he is known today as "the father of medicine." Hippocrates vowed that anything he saw or heard when providing care to the sick would remain private. "I will keep silence," he wrote, "counting on such things to be sacred secrets."

Modern medical care often involves many more people than a doctor and patient. There are also nurses, pharmacists, radiologists, respiratory therapists, insurance processors, and countless others. In fact, a person undergoing care in a hospital can easily expect as many as two hundred people to see his or her records.

With so many people having access to such personal information, trouble is sure to arise. In 1996 Jamie

Grzadzinski, a middle school student, came home with shocking news. She told her parents that another kid, Lorenzo Castellano, had taunted her. He called her an "AIDS baby." Naturally, she wondered why.

Jamie's parents had been hoping to avoid the subject. Her dad had been diagnosed with AIDS three years earlier and was taking drugs to keep the disease stable. He and his wife had chosen not to tell Jamie and her brother. "We just wanted to keep it to ourselves," said Kathy Grzadzinski. "There is such a stigma attached to the word HIV, AIDS. We wanted them to enjoy their life. We wanted to protect them."

So, then, how did Jamie's classmate Lorenzo Castellano know? His mother, Dawn Castellano, was a clerk at the drugstore that filled Stanley Grzadzinski's prescriptions. The Grzadzinskis sued Dawn Castellano and the drugstore for violating patient confidentiality. Castellano denied that she had told her son anything, and Lorenzo denied everything as well. But a witness said otherwise. Eventually, the parties settled the case out of court, rather than in the public forum of a court trial.

In the twenty-first century, such a lapse in privacy is less likely to occur. Under the Health Insurance Portability and Accountability Act of 1996 (HIPAA), medical caregivers are required to protect the privacy of their patients' records. The act does not ensure absolute privacy, however, and it appears to be poorly enforced. Critics also note that HIPAA has created some new problems.

Medical data enjoys one very key distinction from much other personal data. There is clearly a legitimate reason to keep and maintain a person's medical records. These records provide direction for a patient's care throughout his or her life and can even save a patient's life. It is hard to make this argument about such data as a person's searches on Google. At the same time, it is important that each patient be able to access his or her medical records and correct any mistakes. Under HIPAA, Americans have greater access to these records.

MEDICAL PRIVACY? WHAT MEDICAL PRIVACY?

In the early 1970s, a number of insurance data banks maintained medical and personal information on millions of Americans. This information was available to insurance companies and other firms. It helped them decide whom they would insure, extend credit to, or hire. But much of the information they had was inaccurate and based on gossip. What's more, it was off-limits to the subjects of the records. They were the medical patients, insurance policyholders, and people who were applying for medical insurance. A person who suspected his or her medical information was incorrect could not even get access to it in order to check its accuracy. Yet insurance companies and other firms could use the information again and again to make important decisions about that person. One man's insurance file noted that he drank "three martinis before dinner." A woman whose medical records indicated that she had borne a child out of wedlock was marked as having a questionable moral character.

In 1971 the Fair Credit Reporting Act went into effect. It granted individuals access to their credit records as part of the country's effort to grant greater access to personal records. However, the act didn't extend to medical records.

The Medical Information Bureau (MIB), which still exists, supplied information on more than ten million Americans to hundreds of insurance companies. It included not only information about people's medical care but also their drinking habits, hazardous hobbies such as auto racing, and their sex lives. A person seeking insurance had "no way of knowing what is being used against him," said John E. Gregg of the Policyholders Protective Association. "The millions of consumers who have secret information stockpiled in the MIB storehouse should be given an absolute right to know if it is hurting them," said Gregg.

The director of the MIB at that time fiercely resisted such suggestions because "we think it will cost money" and "it won't do the individual any good." Congress disagreed with him, however, and passed an amendment to the Fair Credit Act. The amendment allowed individuals to view and correct, if necessary, records in medical data banks. In the twenty-first century, the MIB maintains basic, coded medical data on millions of patients. An individual can now contact the MIB to check the accuracy of his or her data.

But that was hardly the end of the problems regarding medical privacy, particularly once computers and the Internet came into greater use. Suddenly it was far easier to circulate patient information. Add to that the normal human capacity for making mistakes, and the potential for problems multiplies.

"Many of the worst cases of privacy abuse we have heard [about] are the result of errors, carelessness and poor judgment by those who handle personal information," said Beth Givens of the Privacy Rights Clearinghouse in 1996. "And some are the result of inadequate security in the handling of personal information."

One woman was continually being denied health insurance. After being turned down by a number of companies, she asked to see her records at the Medical Information Bureau. It turned out her file codes showed her to have Alzheimer's and a heart condition, neither of which was correct.

HELLO, HIPAA

Congress took up the issue of medical privacy again in the mid-1990s. It was more than two decades after Congress had passed the Fair Credit Act and its amendment expanding people's access to their medical records. In 1996 Vice President Albert Gore made a speech announcing an "Electronic Bill of Rights" and stressed the need to protect medical records. Soon after, Congress began to hammer out HIPAA.

As originally drafted, HIPAA would have given patients broad control over their medical records. A doctor would have been unable to share a patient's information with anyone without the patient's consent, not even another doctor or insurance company. This consent was referred to as "opting in." Under pressure from the medical community and President George W. Bush, however, HIPAA went into effect in 2003 with an opt-out approach. It gives patients only partial control over how their medical data is used.

When a patient sees a doctor for the first time, he or she is asked to sign a HIPAA form. By signing the form, the patient acknowledges that his or her medical records can be shared with other health-care providers and insurance companies. Medical information cannot be shared with an employer, however, nor used for marketing or advertising that is not health related without the consent of the patient.

In addition, a patient can ask for a copy of his or her medical records. He or she can correct the records, if necessary, and obtain a report on how the medical records were used and with whom they were shared. HIPAA applies to most health-care providers, such as doctors, nurses, hospitals, pharmacies, clinics, health maintenance organizations known as an HMOs, and nursing homes. It also covers health insurance providers and government programs such as

Medicare and Medicaid. Protected patient information includes information a health worker puts in a person's medical records, conversations with doctors and other health workers, billing information, and health insurance data.

HIPAA covers not just written and computerized medical information but also verbal information. Dr. Jeffrey Hausfeld is an ear, nose, and throat doctor who helped to train colleagues on HIPAA requirements. He noted that some of the worst medical privacy violations were apt to occur in a doctor's office.

The doctor offered examples: "You're in the back of the office and you're looking at a patient and you want to call to the front, sometimes you get on the intercom. 'Can you get me Mrs. Smith's biopsy report? I need it right now.' Or somebody calls on the phone and [the receptionist] calls back to you, 'Mr. Jones is on the phone. He wants to know if he can get a renewal of his Prozac prescription.'" Dr. Hausfeld stressed that doctors should keep privacy in mind when handling patient records and charts and discussing their care.

A number of states, such as California, have laws that provide additional medical privacy protection. In 2004, for example, the Privacy Rights Clearinghouse filed a case in California Superior Court against Albertsons, which is a supermarket chain with pharmacies. The privacy rights organization accused Albertsons of illegally using prescription information for marketing purposes, which was a violation of state law. By using its prescription records, Albertsons was contacting its pharmacy customers by mail and over the telephone, urging them to refill their prescriptions or switch to a different medication. Albertsons appeared to be contacting customers out of concern that they keep up their treatment. In actuality, Albertsons received anywhere from three to fifteen

In California in 2004, the Privacy Rights Clearinghouse filed a lawsuit against Albertsons supermarket for using customers' prescription information as a marketing tool.

dollars from pharmaceutical companies each time it contacted a customer.

"This could translate into millions of dollars of income for Albertsons from an unauthorized and unwanted drug marketing scheme which violates medical privacy rights of thousands of Albertsons' customers," said Beth Givens of the Privacy Rights Clearinghouse. It is interesting to note that Albertsons, a huge chain, operates in a number of states with medical privacy laws that are more lenient than California's.

NOT HIGH ON HIPAA

HIPAA does have its share of detractors. Medical researchers, for instance, say that HIPAA has hampered their work. The act's requirement of consent, they say, has greatly reduced the number of patients participating in medical studies. Before HIPAA was enacted, doctors needed only a verbal consent to include a patient in such a study. Under HIPAA, they must obtain a written consent. Unfortunately, potential participants appear to misunderstand the permission forms. "They ask us if they'll have to come in for a blood drawing," said Eva Kline-Rogers, the program manager, " . . . when all we're asking for is permission to call them, ask them how they're doing and put their anonymous data into a database."

Fewer patients is a problem for researchers because they need a large pool of patient volunteers to produce statistically significant results. A large pool of volunteers in a diabetes research study, for instance, is more likely to reflect diabetes trends among the general population than a small group of volunteers.

"HIPAA has made it very difficult to do critical healthcare research where the results would not harm patient privacy in any way," said Edward Goldman, deputy general counsel for the University of Michigan's Cardiovascular Center. The center, which conducts cardiac research, relies on heart-attack patients for their studies on heart-attack care and follow-up care. Prior to HIPAA, 96 percent of heart-attack and chest-pain survivors participated in the center's follow-up surveys. After HIPAA, the percentage sank to 34 percent.

The results of the Michigan program echo those of other medical research programs. "In our opinion, . . . the pendulum has swung too far," said an editorial in the *New England Journal of Medicine*.

"We won't solve safety, quality and cost issues in healthcare unless we do quality research, and our findings show that HIPAA, as currently written, has the potential to hinder that effort," stated Dr. Kim Eagle, clinical director of the University of Michigan's Cardiovascular Center.

Law enforcement officials also have lodged complaints against HIPAA's privacy restrictions. Sergeant Andrew Gallagher of the Stamford, Connecticut, police department was investigating a car accident in which a nine-year-old boy had been injured. When he went to the hospital to check on the boy's condition, the hospital would tell him nothing. The staff refused to even say if the boy was a patient.

Even in cases involving a crime or a suspected crime, police do not always get the information they seek. In Kansas a police chief came to the local hospital looking for two murder suspects who had taken part in a shoot-out. Hospital staffers would not talk to him. "I said, 'Do you want somebody who has just been charged with first-degree murder walking around your city after walking out of your hospital?'" exclaimed Police Chief Dean Akings of Great Bend, Kansas.

MEDICAL PRIVACY IN THE HIPAA ERA

Well after HIPAA went into effect, Americans remained highly concerned about health-care privacy. According to a 2005 study, 67 percent of Americans were concerned about the privacy of their medical information and were unfamiliar with their HIPAA rights. Even worse, one out of eight people surveyed were following unhealthy practices to protect their medical privacy. They sometimes went to someone other than their regular doctor to keep the regular doctor from learning about a medical condition. Some avoided medical tests, or they asked their doctor not to record a medical problem. These practices stem largely from fears that an employer or insurance company will use the medical information against them. In fact, 52 percent are concerned about how employers will use medical information. In a 1999 study, only 36 percent expressed similar worries.

Clinics and medical centers have mistakenly posted personal medical information online, and thieves have made off with computers containing patient records. Medical records still end up in places they should not be. Reporters for a Michigan television station dug into twenty dumpsters located outside physicians' offices. Half the dumpsters contained patient records, which included information about their medical history, their Social Security numbers, and more.

Keeping medical records private is complicated by one more factor. About 10 percent of medical transcription work (transcribing medical reports on computer from handwritten or oral reports) is done far from U.S. shores, in countries such as Pakistan. These countries are beyond the reach of U.S. privacy laws.

As of 2006, Americans had filed 19,420 complaints alleging HIPAA violations. The complaints were filed with the Office of Civil Rights (OCR) in the U.S. Department of Health and Human Services. OCR penalized violators in just two cases. The OCR policy is to urge the accused violators to comply with HIPAA regulations voluntarily. Given the lack of actual penalties, Janlori Goldman, a medical privacy expert, noted, "we're dangerously close to having a law that is essentially meaningless."

CHAPTER 6

PRIVACY ON THE JOB

According to a 2005 survey, more than three-fourths of the country's employers monitor their employees' Internet use. Lest you feel outrage on the part of the employees, however, consider this fact. During the 2006 NCAA (National Collegiate Athletic Association) basketball championship, one study estimated that employers lost about $237 million in productivity from employees who watched the games on the Internet.

In the workplace, an employee's privacy concerns must compete with the company's bottom line, or profits. If an employee is wasting time on the Internet or raising the company's health-care costs by smoking, the company's profits might suffer.

"You should take your passport when you go to work because all your rights as an American citizen disappear the second you walk through the office door," said Lewis Maltby of the National Workrights Institute. Many Americans spend more than one-third of their time at the workplace. Nevertheless, there are fewer privacy laws regulating the workplace than any other area where privacy is a concern. That is probably why the American Civil Liberties Union claims it fields more inquiries about the workplace than any other type of privacy issue.

The concerns generally involve (1) surveillance, in the form of computer monitoring, telephone monitoring, or hidden cameras; (2) lifestyle discrimination, in which the employer makes decisions based on what an employee does outside of the office; and (3) drug testing.

COMPUTER MONITORING

At the Epson Corporation in California, Alana Shoars had always assured employees that their e-mails were private. Hired in 1989 to handle the company's e-mail program, she was in a position to know. Over time, she taught more than seven hundred employees how the e-mail system worked, including the use of passwords. One day she arrived at work to find a manager printing out wads of employee e-mails. Shoars was stunned.

"My policy and procedure is you don't read anything that isn't addressed to you," Shoars said. Shoars, who was fired after challenging the manager's actions, sued the company for violating employees' privacy.

The Epson employees had an expectation of privacy. They had passwords for their e-mail accounts, and Shoars had explained that their communications would be private. Nonetheless, a federal court sided with the company.

Employers, for their part, argue that the question boils down to property rights. The company owns the computers, software, telephones, and other equipment, and they are to be used only for work-related purposes.

Since the Epson case was decided, the law has continued to favor employers in cases concerning workplace privacy. Employers can read employees' e-mails, monitor their computer use, and view their computer terminals. They can listen to phone messages left for employees and phone calls made on company-owned equipment. In California, however, privacy laws require that a person be notified if calls are being monitored or recorded.

According to a 2005 survey by the American Management Association and the ePolicy Institute, about 55 percent of companies save and review employees' e-mails. Twenty-five percent of them have fired employees for e-mail abuse. In addition, 76 percent monitor employees' Internet use, and 26 percent have fired employees for misuse of the Internet.

Some firms, such as Array Networks, in California, are concerned about employees sharing company secrets with business competitors. The company relies on an e-mail filter to catch any secrets in employees' messages. Other firms save e-mail records in case they will need them someday as evidence for lawsuits that involve the company or the employee.

"Workers' e-mail, IM [instant messaging], blog and Internet content creates written business records that are the electronic equivalent of DNA evidence," says Nancy Flynn of the ePolicy Institute. "To help control the risk of litigation [lawsuits], security breaches and other electronic disasters, employers should take advantage of technology tools to battle people problems."

Some companies believe that monitoring employee e-mails hurts morale and undermines trust, however. The policies of the Windber Medical Center in Windber, Pennsylvania, for instance, prohibit employees from sharing pornography via e-mail. But the company does not actually review workers' e-mails. "It's absolutely a trust basis," explains Nicholas Jacobs, the center's chief operating officer. "I haven't been burned yet."

Problems are more likely to occur if employees have a greater expectation of privacy than the laws in their state provide. Employers would do well to set up their systems "so the employees have no expectation of privacy," says Maureen O'Neill, an Atlanta, Georgia, attorney. For instance, they might include a notice in the log-in procedure, reminding employees that e-mail and Internet use may be monitored. The employee handbook should also clearly state the company's policy. By 2005 more than 80 percent of employers notified employees that the company monitors e-mail and Internet activity.

VIDEO SURVEILLANCE

Gail Nelson, a receptionist at the Small Business Development Center at Salem State College, in Massachusetts, had counted on privacy at the office in 1995. That was the year she got such a bad sunburn that she had to apply an ointment several times a day. She would leave her desk and slip into an area at the back of the office. There she would unbutton her blouse and apply the ointment. Sometimes she would change her clothes. It was only later that she learned all of her activity had been captured on camera. Her boss had installed a twenty-four-hour video camera there in an attempt to catch a former client who seemed to be visiting the office without permission after hours. Nelson sued, claiming her boss had violated her privacy.

The Supreme Judicial Court of Massachusetts disagreed. In a unanimous decision, delivered in April 2006, the justices decided, "The office was public." The area in which Nelson changed was accessible to anyone at the center. She simply used it when no one was around. "Despite all of the plaintiff's efforts to discreetly conduct acts of a very personal and private nature in the office, in this case there was no objectively reasonable expectation of privacy," said the court.

The American Civil Liberties Union of Massachusetts criticized the court's decision. It had, said the ACLU, "opened the door to secret video surveillance in the workplace."

Employees who seek out restrooms and changing rooms for privacy are not immune from prying eyes, either. In many cases, courts have upheld an employer's decision to conduct video surveillance in restrooms, including in the stalls.

Consolidated Freightways, a trucking company based in Washington, installed cameras in employee bathrooms to make sure there were no drug sales or drug use. The company argued that it had the right to install the cameras. Its employees were truckers who belonged to the International

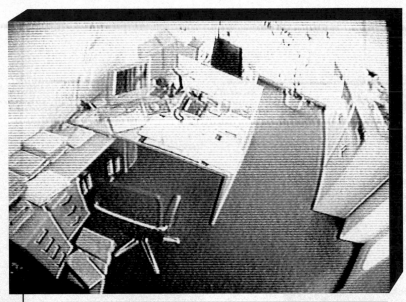

Video monitoring in the workplace is raising questions about how much privacy an employee can expect on the job.

Brotherhood of Teamsters union. The union had agreed to video surveillance in the contract it negotiated with the trucking company. Would the truckers' union representatives have signed the contract if it had specifically granted the company permission to videotape them at the urinals?

A plant manager at Atlas Cold Storage in Pendergrass, Georgia, liked to tell his female employees, "There's not anywhere you can go where I can't see you." Sure enough, he was videotaping them in the bathroom.

Three states—California, New York, and Rhode Island—have laws that prohibit employers from using video surveillance in bathrooms and changing areas. Citizens in the other forty-seven states have little protection. Court decisions have tended to favor employers in video-monitoring cases.

There are cases, however, in which courts have found for employees. When members of the Ontario, California, police department discovered a video camera had been installed in the men's locker room, they sued. The officers claimed that the cameras violated their right to privacy under both federal and state law. In April 2006, the federal court decided the case, *Trujillo v. Ontario*, in favor of the police officers.

BEYOND THE WORKPLACE

What a person does outside of company time is his or her private business or so most people like to think. Employers have been showing more concern about employees' lives outside the workplace, however. They have become increasingly interested in unhealthy habits that may have an impact on their employees' health-care costs. An employee who smokes, for instance, can end up costing the company more in health insurance.

In 2005 a medical benefits provider called Weyco

announced that its employees were not allowed to smoke—
ever. "The main goal is to elevate the health status of our
employees," explained Gary Climes, Weyco's chief financial
officer. Employees must undergo random tests to check for
evidence of smoking. The company also can search an
employee's belongings if he or she is suspected of carrying a
tobacco product. Weyco, which is in Michigan, can fire an
employee who smokes.

About six thousand companies nationwide have similar
policies. Alaska Airlines stopped hiring smokers in 1985, and
its employees must submit to urine tests for nicotine. Such
tests make one wonder: is the airline using the tests to search
for other substances besides nicotine?

A number of privacy advocates, smokers' rights groups, and
employees' rights advocates have spoken out against such
strict antismoking policies. "You're creating a class of
unemployable citizens," says Norman Kjono of a smokers'
rights group.

Overweight employees have come under the employer's
scrutiny too. "If you pay health insurance for your employees,
obesity is your business," says Dr. Thomas Gilliam, coauthor of
the book *Move It. Lose It. Live Healthy: Achieve a Healthier
Workplace One Employee at a Time!* "It directly relates to your
economic health, which affects all of your employees in a very
tangible way."

Some employers have decided to link their employees'
contributions to their health insurance and medical costs with
their willingness to develop healthy habits. It is a way of saving
the company money. The government of King County, in the
state of Washington, is switching to a new program, Healthy
Incentives. It ranks employees into three tiers according to
their health habits. Bronze-level employees—those who

choose not to participate—will pay the highest medical expenses. Silver employees will complete a confidential health assessment and follow one healthy habit. A silver employee might wear a helmet when riding a bicycle or walk for thirty minutes three times a week. Gold employees will complete a confidential assessment, adopt at least two healthy habits, and develop an action plan for improving their health. The program will be run on the honor system. A family that chooses not to participate might pay a $1,500 annual deductible (the amount of medical expenses they must pay before the insurance begins to cover them). A gold family might pay only $300.

"Wellness programs aren't wrong, but they're a very dangerous idea," says Lewis Maltby of the Workplace Rights Institute. "Giving up control of our private lives is too high a price to pay for employers to save a few dollars on health care."

Furthermore, experts ask, where does such an approach end? Could an employer force all employees to use sunscreen or refrain from bungee jumping and riding motorcycles?

More than twenty states have made it illegal for a company to discriminate against employees who smoke. At least one state prohibits employers from discriminating against overweight employees. In addition, a few states protect workers from discrimination for using any legal products, such as alcoholic drinks, or for engaging in legal activities, including dangerous sports.

EMPLOYEE DRUG TESTING

Back in 1983, U.S. employers tested less than 1 percent of their workers for drugs. Today, about half of all U.S. employers, public and private, test their employees for drugs. Almost 70 percent of private firms conduct employee drug tests. Drug testing, under Fourth Amendment law, is considered a search. While there are many laws concerning random drug testing of public employees, there are few laws concerning the testing of private employees.

Drug testing gained wider acceptance under Ronald Reagan, the president of the United States from 1981 to 1989. First Lady Nancy Reagan spearheaded the "Just Say No to Drugs" campaign, and President Reagan supported a range of antidrug legislation. The Drug-Free Workplace Act of 1988, for example, held that federal offices must be drug free. Also, anyone or any firm receiving a grant from the federal government, such as a school or an arts organization, had to be drug free.

Usually, under Fourth Amendment law, a government official, such as a police officer, must have a good reason to suspect a crime has been committed before subjecting an individual to any kind of search. However, the laws regarding drug testing are looser for public employees. They are people who work on behalf of the public and are usually employed by the local, state, or federal government. (A school bus driver, for example, is usually a public employee.) For public employees, routine drug testing is generally considered legal if there is a special need involved. For instance, any public employee whose job affects public safety generally may be tested for drugs.

This standard was set forth by the U.S. Supreme Court in 1989 in two cases, *Skinner v. Railway Labor Executives' Association* and *National Treasury Employees v. von Raab*. The Skinner decision upheld federal regulations for testing railroad employees for drugs. The regulations were enacted in the wake of train accidents in which an employee's drug or alcohol use was a factor. The Supreme Court supported the testing in *National Treasury Employees*, which challenged the drug testing of customs agents. The Court reasoned that many of the agents carry firearms. In order to operate them safely, they could not be under the influence of drugs. In addition, many agents are responsible for finding and taking possession of illegal drugs. Thus, they needed to be able to resist the temptation of using any seized drugs themselves.

The "special needs" standards set forth in these two cases have guided decisions in later cases involving public employees and drug testing. For instance, the courts have upheld the right to test the following people: subway train drivers, anyone involved in aviation, emergency room physicians, government employees with security clearance, prison employees, and anyone involved in intercepting and seizing illegal drugs.

Drug testing by private employers is a different story. Unlike public employers, private firms are virtually free to conduct drug tests at will. They are not bound by Fourth Amendment law.

According to the U.S. Department of Health and Human Services, U.S. firms lose $81 million a year from employees' substance abuse. One drug-testing company, Avitar, claims that drug abusers typically miss far more days of work than those who do not use illegal drugs. Avitar claims drug use results in workplace injuries. It claims that drug testing can reduce these by 51 percent within two years.

Critics of drug testing, on the other hand, contend that the practice fosters an atmosphere of distrust and is a needless expense. They also argue that the tests have an unacceptable error rate.

The American Management Association says there are better alternatives to drug tests. The association believes employers should administer a coordination test, like the one police sometimes administer to someone they suspect of driving while drunk. Yet drug tests continue to be the test of choice.

The Cripple Creek & Victor Gold Mining Company, in Colorado, started random drug testing in 1989. At first, "people thought it was getting into their private life," said one employee, Shawn Tomlinson. "Then they got used to it."

Some workers find drug testing a source of great anxiety. One employee responded anonymously to a government survey about drug testing:

> As an employee of a government contractor I am subject to random drug testing. I have been tested for drugs about ten times in the last five years. After each drug test it takes several days to get the results. Since I do not use drugs the only way a test could turn up positive is if I ate something or used a medication that somehow causes a positive result. But since the consequences of a positive drug test are the immediate destruction of my career, I stay worried and distracted until the results arrive. Your random drug testing program has been very effective in preventing drug use, but has unfortunately destroyed what could have been a healthy, respectful, and productive relationship between employees and management. . . . Now you propose to subject us to hair, saliva and sweat testing [for drugs]. I think I will just leave. My talents and hard work as an engineer, and my happiness and physical and mental health are too valuable to waste in an environment like this.

Thelma Arnold, shown here with her dog, Dudley, was surprised to learn that she was one of hundreds of thousands of America Online (AOL) customers whose searches were posted online by the Internet company.

CHAPTER 7

DATA, DATA EVERYWHERE: PRIVACY AND COMMERCIAL DATA

When the phone rang in Thelma Arnold's home in August 2006, she surely was not expecting to find a *New York Times* reporter on the other end of the line. The reporter had a surprising question for her: was she the America Online (AOL) user who, in the spring of 2006, had conducted hundreds of searches? One search was for "numb fingers," for example, and another was for "homes sold in Shadow Lake subdivision"?

"Those are my searches," Arnold replied. Her searches were among twenty million searches conducted by 658,000 AOL subscribers over a three-month period. AOL had posted the searches online for researchers who study Internet use.

To protect members' identities, AOL had assigned each subscriber a number and then grouped each subscriber's searches together. Each group of searches provided a mini-profile of the user. For instance, member number 4417749 had searched for people with the last name Arnold and "landscapers in Lilburn, Georgia." As a result, the *Times* reporters had little trouble identifying Thelma Arnold. She was a sixty-two-year-old widow who lived in Lilburn, Georgia.

Shocked that AOL had compiled and listed the information, Arnold exclaimed, "My goodness, it's my whole personal life. I had no idea somebody was looking over my shoulder."

AOL was sharply criticized by the media, bloggers, AOL subscribers, and privacy advocates. It quickly withdrew the data from public view. "It was a mistake, and we apologize," the company said in a statement.

For years, privacy advocates had been warning about the possibility of this sort of privacy breach. Many website operators collect data every time someone clicks on their site. These operators include retailers such as Amazon, such search engines as Google, and any website that tracks visitors. They know what pages a person visited, how long he or she viewed each page, the searches the person conducted, and what on-site purchases he or she made. The operators usually save all that data.

This kind of data collection goes on in virtually every avenue of commercial life. "We leave a wake of electronic bits behind with every transaction we make," said Paul Saffo, director of the Institute of the Future. It doesn't take long for that "wake of electronic bits" to swell to the size of an ocean.

There are arguments for maintaining some of this data. On the Internet, "cookies," the same software that collects user information, also saves customers time. It allows them to make purchases without having to reenter their addresses and billing information every time, for example.

There are disturbing aspects to the massive amount of

consumer data that is gathered on the Internet too. Data brokers can buy it, combine it with other data, both private and public, and build highly detailed customer profiles. Then they can sell these profiles to marketing and research firms, prospective potential employers, and even law enforcement officials. Consumer data very often includes high-risk information such as Social Security and bank account numbers. However, the data can be inaccurate. In addition, the more data that is collected, shared, and sold, the more vulnerable the consumer is to identity theft. In 2005 ChoicePoint, one of the country's largest data brokers, reported that it had mistakenly sold the personal financial records of more than 163,000 consumers to criminals intent on committing identity theft.

According to a 2006 poll, more people are worried about having their identities stolen than they are about getting cancer, being the victim of a violent crime, or being harmed in a terrorist attack.

At the heart of all this data collection lie several fundamental questions: First and foremost, who owns all this data? Does it belong to the person to whom the data refers, such as the customer? Or does it belong to the company that collected it? Also, what right do commercial interests—for example, retailers, banks, credit card companies, and Internet service providers—have to retain all that data? Finally, what, if any, laws are in place to protect consumer privacy?

THE NOT-SO-GOOD OLD DAYS

The collection of personal data is nothing new. Long before the existence of personal computers and the Internet, companies gathered data on consumers and sold the information. In the 1960s, credit bureaus maintained mountains of information about millions of citizens. The Retail Credit Company, for instance, compiled files on 45 million Americans. Insurance agencies, credit companies, and employers used the files to make important decisions about a person's eligibility for insurance, credit, and employment.

To gather information, Retail Credit hired thousands of "field representatives," who, in some ways, were just plain snoops. For instance, the company would send around "welcome neighbor" hostesses to visit newcomers in town. The hostesses would pump the newcomers for information, which was fed into the company's files. One file described a family's son as a "hippie-type youth" who was "suspected of using marijuana." His family was turned down for car insurance, based on remarks like these. In this case, they were not even true.

The Retail Credit Company's files "contain information that covers an individual's job, associations, marital situation, personal habits and background gossip drawn from neighbors or anyone willing to talk to the credit bureau's investigator," said the consumer advocate Ralph Nader in 1971. Not only did the data include gossipy tidbits and false impressions, sometimes basic facts were just plain wrong. For instance, a salary might be listed incorrectly, an error that could keep a person from obtaining credit.

But under the laws of that time, consumers were not allowed to see their files. Since they had no access to their personal data, they could not correct any errors. Eventually, in 1970, Congress passed the Fair Credit Reporting Act. It forced the credit bureaus to change their practices and give consumers the opportunity to review their records. In the twenty-first century, an individual can obtain one free copy of his or her credit report per year and request corrections.

Since 1970 Congress has addressed other consumer privacy issues, but not in a systematic way. It has enacted privacy legislation in reaction to court rulings, for example. In 1976 the Supreme Court decided the case *United States v. Miller*. Mitch Miller, a bootlegger, was suspected of failing to pay his taxes. The Bureau of Alcohol, Tobacco and Firearms (part of the U.S. Treasury Department at the time) asked Miller's bank for his records. Without notifying Miller, the bank gave the federal agents the information. Miller claimed that the information was protected by the Fourth Amendment. The Supreme Court disagreed.

Congress believed that the Supreme Court ruled incorrectly. As a result, Congress passed the Right to Financial Privacy Act (RFPA). Under the act, a bank cannot give an agent of the federal government access to a customer's financial records without first notifying the customer and giving him a chance to object.

The headlines have provided another inspiration for new privacy laws. In 1987 President Ronald Reagan nominated Judge Robert Bork to fill a vacancy on the U.S. Supreme Court. Bork was a controversial choice, primarily because he maintained that there was no such thing as a legal right to privacy. A reporter at *City Paper*, a hip Washington, D.C., weekly, put Bork's position to a test. He walked into Bork's favorite video store and asked for a list of titles Bork had rented. Then the reporter published the list in *City Paper*. If Bork was not willing to protect privacy, reasoned the reporter, then he should not mind everyone knowing what he liked to watch in the privacy of his own home.

Bork was rejected as a Supreme Court justice, but the list of videos got the nation's attention. Congressional leaders were appalled that such a list was so easily obtained. Hence, they passed the Video Privacy Protection Act of 1988. The act is "one of the strongest protections of consumer privacy against

Supreme Court nominee Robert Bork testified during confirmation hearings in 1987. A reporter's successful attempt to obtain Bork's video rental history eventually resulted in the passage of the Video Privacy Protection Act.

a specific form of data collection," according to the Electronic Privacy Information Center. The law makes it illegal to disclose a person's rental data without his or her consent. Police officers need a warrant before they can obtain a person's video or DVD rental history.

OPT IN OR OPT OUT?

The Video Privacy Protection Act and Right to Financial Privacy Act are noteworthy in that they give the individual control over his or her records. The individual must give consent before his or her data is shared. The issue of consent has been one of the most controversial aspects of enacting new privacy laws. The story of the Gramm-Leach-Bliley Act (GLBA), also known as the Financial Services Modernization Act of

1999, illustrates how this issue can play out.

Congress enacted the Gramm-Leach-Bliley Act to allow financial institutions more freedom to merge, so that two medium-size institutions could form one very large one. Under the GLBA, a bank can merge with an insurance company or a brokerage company. After a few mergers, the result might be a huge financial megabusiness. Such a massive company would house lots and lots of customer data.

Congressional leaders were concerned about how these large financial institutions would protect their customers' data. When legislators crafted the GLBA, they considered different protective measures. They chose what is referred to as an "opt-out" regulation. Under an opt-out standard, it is up to the customer to tell the bank not to share his or her data with firms such as marketing companies. What this means, however, is that any customer who does not make the effort to opt out is assumed to have granted the bank permission to do as it chooses with the data.

Most banks notify customers of their right to opt out by including an enclosure in a monthly bank statement. The notices are often written in small print. They generally use legal terminology that can easily overwhelm the average customer. Privacy advocates say such notices are usually tossed out. They prefer an opt-in provision. Under an opt-in system, customers would have to expressly give permission before a financial institution could share their personal information.

In North Dakota, the GLBA created a major controversy. Until Congress passed GLBA, financial data about the state's citizens had been governed by the state's opt-in standard. After the passage of GLBA, state officials decided to follow federal opt-out standards instead. That decision didn't sit well with a number of North Dakota folks. A group called Protect Our

Privacy circulated a petition calling for a return to the opt-in standard. The issue ended up on the state ballot in 2002. It was the first time American voters were given the chance to vote on the issue.

Members of the Constitution Party urged North Dakota voters to choose the opt-in standard. They believed that private information was the voters' property and they should not have to go to great lengths to protect it. Bankers and financial institutions, on the other hand, spent a small fortune opposing the opt-in movement. They claimed that the opt-in model would hurt business growth. One ad, which was eventually pulled, went so far as to say that customers would no longer be able to use ATM cash machines if the state adopted the provision (which wasn't true).

Nearly three-fourths of the people in North Dakota who voted in 2002 chose to return to the opt-in standard, exerting tighter control over their personal data. At the core of this controversy was the question, who owns personal data? The voters' emphatic answer was "We do!"

DO THEY KNOW YOU? INTERNET PRIVACY

Imagine an opt-in Internet. When a visitor first arrived at a website, a prompt would appear asking if the website operator could collect and store data from the visit. But that's not how it works in real life. Many websites keep a record of every keystroke, every search term, and every click linked to a visitor's Internet Protocol (IP) address, which is basically a computer's address. Then they store this data. In some cases, they sell it.

In the early days of the Internet, the World Wide Web was a fairly anonymous place. Then along came cookies, developed in 1994. Cookies enabled website operators to track their users.

They could track what users clicked on and, in the case of online retailers, what they bought.

"Before cookies, the Web was essentially private," noted Lawrence Lessig, a professor at Stanford Law School. "After cookies, the Web becomes a space capable of extraordinary monitoring." In fact, early on, the use of cookies caused a furor among privacy advocates.

"My first reaction was, 'Oh they're terrible!'" admitted Richard M. Smith of the Privacy Foundation. "[A]s I've looked at the Internet and how it works, it would be very difficult to have the Internet without them," he added. In other words, many people feel that the benefits of cookies are worth the loss of privacy they create—at least up to a point. It is convenient to be able to order from a favorite online retailer without having to enter credit card and shipping information with every new order. But what about all the other information cookies collect?

If a website operator isn't careful, all that stored information could create problems for users or the website operator or both. Such was the case when AOL posted its subscribers' searches on the Internet, including those of Thelma Arnold, who was contacted by a *New York Times* reporter. The episode brought vividly to light the sort of violation privacy advocates had been warning of for years. "It's only by these kinds of screw-ups and unintended behind-the-curtain views that we can push this dialogue thing along," said John Battelle, author of *The Search: How Google and Its Rivals Rewrote the Rules of Business and Transformed Our Culture*. "As unhappy as I am to see this data on people leaked," he said, "I'm heartened that we will have this conversation as a culture, which is long overdue."

In fact, the episode did generate discussion and gave concrete form to what had previously been mostly theoretical questions.

One hotly debated issue was whether law enforcement agencies should be granted access to search engine data.

Although many of the AOL searches seemed harmless, there were plenty of a more troubling nature. One AOL subscriber, for instance, spent an hour running searches on how to kill a wife.

What would happen if AOL had shared the man's information with a law enforcement agency? Would the agency be justified in investigating him? On the other hand, would anybody ever conduct searches for anything that sounded the least bit suspicious if they knew the government was watching? "The public should not be afraid of searching for any information, no matter how personal and private it may be," said Aden Fine of the American Civil Liberties Union.

The AOL debacle does not appear to have altered any companies' policies. Google, for instance, plans to keep storing user queries. "We are reasonably satisfied . . . that this sort of thing would not happen at Google," said Eric Schmidt, Google's chief executive officer, "although you can never say never."

Just a few months before AOL posted its subscribers' data, the U.S. Justice Department tried to subpoena Google's search records (require Google to turn the records over to the courts or face a penalty) in an effort to crack down on child pornography. Google fought the subpoena on the grounds that turning over the data would violate its customers' privacy. In the end, the court ordered Google to turn over a small slice of data.

LEGISLATING INTERNET PRIVACY

At this time, no broad federal law protects citizens' privacy online. In fact, the authors of the report "Protecting Consumers Online" noted that federal law reserves "our strongest privacy protections for cable and video records, while travel records and online purchasing data are left disturbingly vulnerable."

The Children's Online Privacy Protection Act (COPPA), which took effect in 2000, protects children's online data. Under COPPA, companies operating a website must meet certain standards to protect young users. In particular, the Web operator must require a child under the age of thirteen to get parental consent before submitting personal data online. Businesses must also protect the information they have collected online from children.

Congressional representatives have introduced a number of bills pertaining to online privacy. One requires website operators to destroy out-of-date data containing personal information. Some bills focus specifically on cracking down on the use of spyware, software that collects user information without the user's knowledge. Consumer and privacy advocates argue, however, that what is needed is a comprehensive law.

The job of writing such a law raises a lot of tricky questions: Who owns the data? How may it be used? How long can a company maintain the data? Will websites have to adopt an opt-in approach, or can they continue to operate under the current opt-out standard? Will federal law provide minimum Internet privacy protections but allow states to enact even stricter laws? Or will the federal law serve as the final word on Internet privacy?

In addition to addressing these issues, any new comprehensive law will have to be flexible enough to adapt to new technology. Trying to figure out what that new technology might be is a challenge. Who knew, one hundred years ago, that people would one day talk on cell phones or communicate via computer?

▮PART III

On September 11, 2001, a terrorist organization hijacked four airplanes and flew two of them into the towers of the World Trade Center in New York. The U.S. government's reaction to this tragedy caused people to think about whether or not the right to privacy could protect criminals.

CHAPTER 8

PRIVACY AND THE WAR ON TERROR

In early September 2001, privacy made the front page of the *New York Times*. The *Times* ran a three-part article, "Tracks in Cyberspace," about privacy issues in this high-tech era. The series reflected the public's growing discomfort over how personal information was being used. A poll conducted by Hart-Teeter showed that 53 percent of respondents were extremely concerned about loss of privacy. Another third described themselves as quite concerned.

Days later, privacy—and nearly everything else—was pushed off the front page of every major newspaper in the country. On September 11, 19 Arab men connected with al-Qaeda, a terrorist organization, hijacked four commercial airplanes. They flew two planes into New York City's two World Trade Center towers and one into the Pentagon in Washington, D.C. A fourth plane crashed into a field near Shanksville,

Pennsylvania. Almost three thousand people were killed in the attacks. The World Trade Center towers, the most visible buildings in the city's skyline, were wiped off the face of the earth. In addition, much of the country's sense of well-being was destroyed in that one horrific morning.

Suddenly citizens were buying gas masks and generators for electricity. They bought so many American flags that Wal-Mart ran out of them. Schools that had restricted students' cell phone use changed their rules so that anxious parents could easily reach their children. Major League Baseball suspended play for well over a week.

Enemy attacks on the United States have spurred the nation's leaders to take drastic steps in the name of national security. One example occurred during World War II (1939–1945). After the Japanese attack on the U.S. naval base at Pearl Harbor, Hawaii, on December 7, 1941, President Franklin D. Roosevelt signed an executive order. Approximately 120,000 people of Japanese descent were required to leave their homes and businesses and move to relocation camps in remote parts of the country. This massive forced migration was done in the name of national security. Two-thirds of the internees were U.S. citizens.

Like the attack on Pearl Harbor, the 9/11 attacks prompted the country's leaders to take radical steps. Soon after 9/11, the Bush administration drafted a sweeping antiterrorist bill aimed at preventing further attacks. Congressional leaders, who were just as eager to thwart the enemy, chose to take a more careful approach. Most legislators were wary of pushing through major legislation without thorough debate. Despite the president's eagerness to see legislation passed, Congress methodically discussed the issues involved. Then, in early October 2001, a bioterrorism scare sent Capitol Hill into chaos. A Senate staff member had opened an envelope filled with white powder, which contained potentially deadly anthrax spores. (Anthrax is a bacterial disease.) The House and Senate office buildings were closed for days so offices could be checked for anthrax contamination.

The threat of bioterrorism seemed to light a fire under the legislators. By the end of October, with little discussion, they had passed the USA PATRIOT Act. The act incorporated most of the Bush administration's earlier legislation.

The name USA PATRIOT Act is actually an acronym. It stands for Uniting and Strengthening America by Providing Appropriate Tools Required to Intercept and Obstruct Terrorism Act. The PATRIOT Act covered a range of issues. Much of it, however, served to increase the federal government's legal right

President George W. Bush *(seated)* signed the USA PATRIOT Act on October 26, 2001. The bill gives the U.S. government more freedom to conduct surveillance in the hopes of obtaining information to fight terrorism. The Act's opponents, however, felt the Act would erode Americans' civil liberties, including the right to privacy. The bill was re-signed in 2006.

to conduct surveillance. Title II of the act, for instance, gave the federal government "authority to intercept wire, oral, and electronic communications relating to terrorism."

"I think this is the most dramatic modernization of prosecutorial and police powers that Congress has ever passed," said the House Judiciary Committee chairman F. James Sensenbrenner Jr., a Republican from Wisconsin. People concerned about civil liberties, though, claimed the PATRIOT Act threatened basic civil rights. "This legislation is based on the faulty assumption that safety must come at the expense of civil liberties," noted Laura W. Murphy of the American Civil Liberties Union.

THE WAR ON TERROR VERSUS PRIVACY

In the months that followed, the Bush administration introduced new antiterrorism initiatives. Many of these initiatives asked the public to give up some privacy in the name of fighting al-Qaeda. The U.S. Justice Department came up with Operation TIPS, short for Terrorism Information and Prevention System. Operation TIPS would give "millions of American truckers, letter [mail] carriers, train conductors, ship captains, utility employees, and others a formal way to report suspicious terrorist activity," noted the government's website. They would be trained to "serve as extra eyes and ears for law enforcement." For instance, a trucker might notice and report a vacant truck parked under a bridge—a truck that might be filled with explosives.

Critics were quick to point out the program's flaws. "Police cannot routinely enter people's houses without either permission or a warrant," noted the *Washington Post* in an editorial. "They should not be using utility workers to conduct surveillance they could not lawfully conduct themselves."

The *Boston Globe* was more direct. "Operation TIPS," it declared in an editorial, "is a scheme that Joseph Stalin would have appreciated." (Stalin was a brutal dictator of the former Soviet Union.) Others argued that TIPS would be ineffective. "What you're going to get is a lot of phone calls about an Arab couple who moved down the street and everyone is suspicious," said counterterrorism expert Juliette Kayyem.

One delivery person, Butch Traylor, said that he and his fellow workers had "donated time and money to support the victims" of 9/11, but "a program that asks people like us to do surveillance is a dangerous overreaction." Postal service workers also declined to participate. Eventually, Operation TIPS was scrapped.

Despite the public outcry about government initiatives such as TIPS, the country had hardly returned to its pre-9/11 mind-set. A year after the terrorist attacks, people spoke of living in a "post-9/11 world."

In November 2002, Congress easily passed a major antiterrorism bill, the Homeland Security Act. This 484-page piece of legislation consolidated twenty-two existing federal agencies into a new cabinet-level agency, the Department of Homeland Security. The creation of the Department of Homeland Security was the most massive restructuring of the U.S. government since the formation of the Department of Defense after World War II. Among the agencies Homeland Security included were the Transportation Security Administration, the Immigration and Naturalization Service, Federal Emergency Management Agency, and parts of the Justice Department and the FBI. Homeland Security would be responsible for securing the country's borders, preventing terrorist attacks, and creating a national defense strategy. It would also respond to disasters, both natural and human-made.

In terms of privacy issues, experts gave the act mixed reviews. On the plus side, the act forbade the creation of the TIPS program. It also created a privacy ombudsman (complaints manager) within the Department of Homeland Security. The ombudsman would evaluate whether new programs threatened people's privacy and civil liberties. On the other hand, the new act limited how much information citizens could request under the Freedom of Information Act. The law was passed in 1966 to grant Americans access to government records.

One area in which the effects of 9/11 were still keenly felt was air travel. Since the attacks, airline passengers had coped with new requirements such as removing their shoes at the security gate. Many passengers continued to feel an increased wariness in the sky. "Some people are so very, very nervous," said Steve Kemble, a frequent flier. "In first class, any time anyone comes up from the back, all of a sudden everybody becomes more guarded."

Air travel, it seemed, would be a natural target for new security measures. Yet a new initiative by the Transportation Security Administration (TSA) to conduct background checks on airline passengers ran into stiff opposition. It was called CAPPS II (Computer Assisted Passenger Pre-Screening system) and was built on CAPPS I. This was an older antiterrorism initiative developed after a terrorist attack on the World Trade Center in 1993. The new program would search passengers' personal records, including their credit and insurance records, to look for any unusual activity. Then the program would categorize passengers by color—green, yellow, or red—according to their perceived security risk. The screening was intended to reduce time-consuming pat downs by airport

Airline passengers going through an airport security checkpoint must remove their shoes and place them and their other belongings in bins to be scanned. After the terrorist attacks on September 11, 2001, airport security has become stronger in the hopes of preventing another such attack.

screeners. The screeners sometimes pat a passenger's body to check for banned materials such as weapons. Pat downs and other security measures had become so bothersome that many travelers had opted to drive rather than fly to their destinations

When the TSA enlisted Delta Airlines to test the program, many Delta customers decided to boycott the airline. In a *Washington Post* survey, business travelers gave CAPPS "a resounding thumbs down." "I will make it a point to avoid Delta or any other airline which intrudes into my personal life simply because I choose to fly with that airline," responded one *Post* reader, James G. Rickey Others were concerned about what such background checks would turn up. For instance, would the airline refuse passage to a father who was behind on his child-support payments?

Some indicated they were in favor of the program if it meant a speedier trip through security, but they were in the minority. A survey conducted by the Association of Corporate Travel Executives found that 82 percent of the 255 people surveyed considered CAPPS II to be an invasion of privacy. Seventy-nine percent said the program would discourage travelers from choosing a participating airline. CAPPS II, like TIA and TIPS, was eventually shelved.

HOW FAR IS TOO FAR?

In the spring of 2004, a new survey by Hart-Teeter showed that less than half of all Americans felt safer than they had been before 9/11. Three-fourths expected a major terrorist attack, in the United States or abroad, in the coming months. Would they sacrifice some privacy to help in the war on terror? Maybe and maybe not. Fifty-nine percent said the government should have access to the data of private companies if it would help prevent terrorism. On the other hand, only 27 percent of the respondents trusted the government to use the information properly. Fifty-six percent said the PATRIOT Act was good for the country, but 33 percent said it was bad, and 11 percent were unsure. In other words, people had a lot of different ideas about the war on al-Qaeda and where their privacy figured into the equation.

In December 2005, the *New York Times* broke the news that the government had been conducting massive surveillance, without warrants, on millions of average Americans in the name of combating terrorism. According to reports, President Bush had authorized the program, which allowed the National Security Agency (NSA) to monitor millions of citizens' e-mails and telephone calls. In fact, major telecommunications companies such as AT&T had collaborated with the program.

The reports pushed the highly secretive NSA into the

spotlight. While most Americans are familiar with the Central Intelligence Agency (CIA) and the FBI, far fewer are familiar with the NSA. It is, however, by far the country's largest and best-funded intelligence-gathering organization.

President Harry S. Truman created the NSA in 1952 to spy on foreign enemies by intercepting (basically, secretly listening in on) their communications. He established the NSA simply by signing a top-secret memorandum calling for its creation. (Most federal agencies are established after congressional debate and approval.) For years, the NSA was nicknamed "No Such Agency." However, its power as an intelligence-gathering agency has been unrivaled.

The National Security Agency "has technological capabilities for eavesdropping beyond imagination," wrote James Bamford in his 1982 book about the NSA, *The Puzzle Palace*. As early as the mid-1970s, Senator Frank Church, a Democrat from Idaho, remarked that if the NSA's capabilities were turned on U.S. citizens, "no American would have any privacy left, such is [NSA's] capability to monitor everything: telephone conversations, telegrams, it doesn't matter. There would be no place to hide." Should a dictator take over the country, the NSA "could enable [the government] to impose total tyranny, and there would be no way to fight back."

The NSA operates under different rules than most intelligence-gathering and law enforcement agencies. For foreign-intelligence operations, it needs no court approval. The Constitution does not apply outside the country's borders. To spy on suspects in the United States, however, the NSA must obtain a warrant from the special Foreign Intelligence Surveillance Court (FISC, also known as FISA Court)—a special court prescribed in the Foreign Intelligence Surveillance Act (FISA) of 1978. The act was set in place to oversee the surveillance and collection of foreign intelligence. FISA established the rules under which the NSA can seek warrants from the FISA court. The NSA can obtain a warrant from the FISA Court to spy on suspects in the United States only after showing probable cause, that is, a reason to suspect wrongdoing.

According to media reports, President Bush had directed the NSA to eavesdrop on millions of Americans without the FISA Court's approval. President Bush maintained that his actions were legal under the president's wartime powers. He cited a statute—the Authorization for use of Military Force—passed by Congress in 2001. The American Civil Liberties Union disagreed. It filed a federal lawsuit against the National Security Agency to end the surveillance program on the grounds that it was unconstitutional.

In the spring of 2006, just a few months after the *New York Times* first published a story about the National Security Agency's surveillance program, the NSA made front-page headlines again. The agency had put together an enormous database of two trillion telephone calls. It then sifted through the phone data to find terrorists. The database was gathered from Americans' phone records dating back to 2001. Once again, the legality of such a program came into question. Many asked, just where did the line between consumer privacy and government interests lie? Were there any boundaries at all? Could or should the government have the right to access any and all of its citizens' personal data in the name of national security?

A *Washington Post*–ABC poll found that 63 percent of Americans considered the NSA program an acceptable way to investigate terrorism. In fact, 44 percent strongly supported it. Another 35 percent found the program to be unacceptable. Of those, 24 percent strongly objected to it.

Many technology experts contended that the NSA's data-mining efforts, legal or not, would not lead the agency to terrorists. "Data mining works best when you're searching for a well-defined profile," wrote technology and privacy expert Bruce Schneier. "Credit card fraud is one of data-mining's success stories: All credit-card companies mine their transaction databases for data for spending patterns that indicate a stolen card." Patterns identifying terrorists are not as easy to construct. "It's a needle-in-a-haystack problem," Schneier explained, "and throwing more hay on the pile doesn't make that problem any easier."

Could the database perhaps identify social networks (groups of people who know one another) that would lead the NSA to terrorists? Not likely, according to Valdis Krebs, an expert on using data mining and social networks. He pointed out, "Patterns alone won't tell you whether someone's good or evil."

THWARTED ATTACK

On August 10, 2006, British authorities announced that they had uncovered a terrorist plot. The terrorists planned to use liquid explosives, tucked in their carry-on luggage, to blow up as many as ten U.S. bound passenger jets. Authorities had discovered the plot after following up on a tip from a resident of a Muslim community in London.

In the United States, airports quickly prohibited passengers from bringing aboard virtually any kind of liquid or gel, from toothpaste to bottled water. They made exceptions only for baby formula and prescription medicines. The Department of Homeland Security put the country on a code-red alert, the highest alert level.

The episode was a stark reminder of how vulnerable Americans felt after 9/11. It appeared to have little effect on their opinions concerning government surveillance, however.

Just a week after the terrorist plot was uncovered, a federal judge ruled on the ACLU's case challenging the National Security Agency's surveillance program. Judge Anna Taylor Diggs found that the program violated the First and Fourth Amendments. She also held that it failed to meet the requirements of the Foreign Intelligence Surveillance Act. The Bush administration appealed. Soon after, the House passed legislation granting President Bush the power to conduct the warrantless searches. Supporters claimed the bill's opponents didn't want to protect the country. Opponents said the bill would give the president and all future presidents "a blank check" to do as he or she wished.

REAL ID

One of the facts about the 9/11 attacks that people found most maddening was that the terrorists had obtained state driver's licenses. They had used them to open bank accounts, rent cars, and take flying lessons. In order to prevent such disastrous security errors, federal officials argued, the country had to improve its methods of properly identifying people through passports and driver's licenses.

A result was a controversial measure called the Real ID Act. The act, which Congress passed in May 2005, sets forth new federal requirements for getting a driver's license, regardless of the state in which an applicant lives. The act is an effort to create a nationally uniform system of identification. When the bill goes into effect in December 2009, a U.S. citizen will need to produce the federally approved license not just to drive but also to get on an airplane, enter a federal building, or accept a federal benefit, such as Social Security payments. If a state fails to comply with the act when issuing driver's licenses, then its citizens will be unable to do those things.

As things stand, each state's department of motor vehicles operates independently, and their licensing requirements vary. For example, most require an applicant to prove that he or she is a legal resident, but some do not. A Florida driver's license includes three photos. Others, such as Maryland's, use just one.

Under the Real ID Act, applicants will have to produce as many as five pieces of identification before getting a license. The state will then be required to verify that the documents are authentic. It will copy them and download them to a database that can be accessed by other state motor vehicle departments. The license is expected to include a computer chip, such as an RFID chip or a bar code. It will also probably include a biometric form of identification, such as a fingerprint. The act authorizes the secretary of Homeland Security to add any requirements he or she thinks are necessary.

"The 9/11 hijackers used multiple driver's licenses and birth certificates . . . to live openly in the United States while they planned their deadly attacks," said Jeff Lungren, spokesperson for Representative F. James Sensenbrenner Jr., the bill's sponsor. "Real ID is an effort to prevent that from ever occurring again," Lungren said.

The act has generated strong opposition, though. State governments claim it will cost them billions of dollars to implement. Consumer advocates argue that, given the costs the act will impose on state governments, drivers will end up paying steep fees for a license.

Opponents also question the feasibility of requiring so many forms of identification. "What do you do with people on the Gulf Coast, where so many records were lost?" asked Matthew Dunlap, Maine's secretary of state. (He was referring to the destruction caused by Hurricane Katrina in 2005.) Pamela Walsh, spokesperson for Governor John Lynch, of New

Hampshire, warned that the act would turn "our Department of Motor Vehicle workers into agents for the Department of Homeland Security."

The Real ID Act has also raised substantial privacy concerns from a wide swath of Americans. Conservative organizations have challenged it, as well as civil liberties groups. Republicans have objected along with Democrats. Republican state representative Toby Nixon, in the state of Washington, said the data-linking requirement would amount to "a national citizenship database." He said, "The purpose of the driver's license is to ensure highway safety, not to act as a national ID card." In New Hampshire, state representative Neal M. Kurk, a Republican, told fellow legislators, "We care more for our liberties than to meekly hand over to the federal government the potential to enumerate, track, identify and eventually control" its citizens.

Barry Steinhardt, of the American Civil Liberties Union, protested, "[The Real ID Act is] going to result in everyone, from the 7-Eleven store to the bank and airlines, demanding to see the ID card. They're going to scan it in. It's going to be not just a national ID card but a national database." In light of a number of major recent thefts of government data, some opponents have worried that Real ID is setting up citizens for more identify theft.

The Real ID Act also would indicate a major shift in power from the states to the federal government, violating the federalist foundations on which the country was founded. All in all, the act has a lot of state officials up in arms. Major state government organizations, such as the National Governors Association, challenged the terms of the act in a 2006 report. In January 2007, Maine's state legislature voted to refuse to participate in the Real ID program. Arkansas and Idaho passed similar legislation in March. Comparable legislation is pending in many other states.

Supporters of the Real ID Act remain unmoved. "Any state that's opting out is opting out in doing their part in solving these national challenges," said Representative Dana Rohrabacher, a Republican from California, "and I don't have any sympathy for them." The Coalition for a Secure Driver's License notes that "an insecure system of ID is an invitation to terrorists, drug smugglers, illegal aliens and others to use fake documents as a way to evade the law." One al-Qaeda terrorist had obtained five Michigan licenses in thirteen months. In New York, one Social Security number was used to obtain fifty-seven driver's licenses. A foreigner who was living in Florida illegally presented a driver's license to start work in a nuclear power plant. Could a terrorist do the same thing?

WHAT'S AHEAD

September 11, 2001, triggered a national tug-of-war. Privacy and civil liberties advocates were on one side. Supporters of President Bush and his antiterrorist policies were on the other. In the years since then, at least some of the president's supporters have come to question and even oppose some of his security measures. The September 2006 vote in the House of Representatives that authorized President Bush to conduct warrantless searches was revealing. Thirteen Republicans voted with the Democrats, who largely opposed the measure. On the other hand, seventeen Democrats supported the searches. The vote illustrated how conflicted the country continues to be about how to balance privacy and security.

Benjamin Franklin once said, "They that can give up essential liberty to obtain a little temporary safety deserve neither liberty nor safety." Would he have made an exception to protect the nation from al-Qaeda?

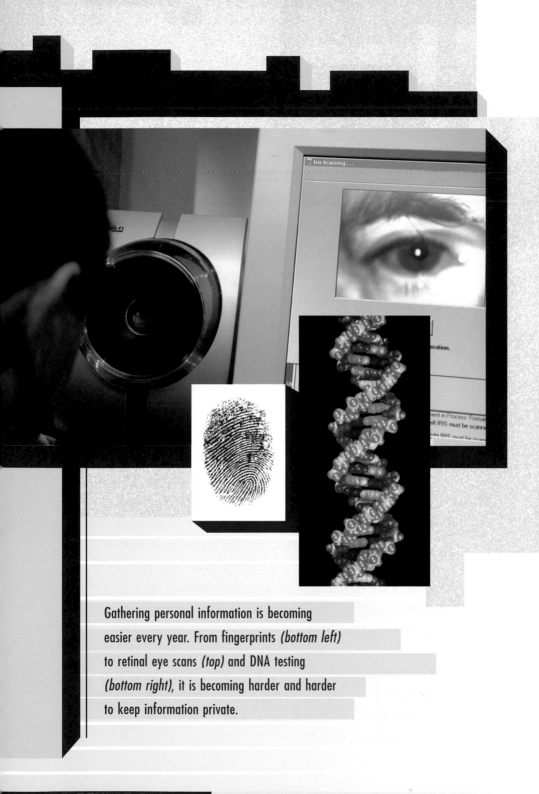

Gathering personal information is becoming easier every year. From fingerprints *(bottom left)* to retinal eye scans *(top)* and DNA testing *(bottom right)*, it is becoming harder and harder to keep information private.

CONCLUSION

Is Privacy Going, Going, Gone?

According to some people, privacy is in its dying stages. For instance, in a report released in 2003, the American Civil Liberties Union warned, "We are at risk of turning into a Surveillance Society." The world envisioned by George Orwell in *1984*, in which Big Brother sees all and knows all, seemed to be on the verge of becoming a reality.

Is this just alarmist talk, or is it true? Consider the evidence provided in these chapters. Surveillance cameras have come into wide use. Some city governments want to link their municipal cameras with cameras in private businesses to create an enormous surveillance network. Aerial cameras can zero in on a private citizen's backyard. It is becoming easier by the day to find detailed images of neighborhoods and homes.

The biometric technology industry, which includes such things as fingerprint and retinal identification devices, is growing like Jack's beanstalk. One marketing report predicts that fingerprint technology alone will grow from a $427.4 million industry in 2004 to a $6.3 billion one by 2012. The same trend is obvious in the use of DNA tests. States are demanding that law enforcement officials take DNA samples from an ever greater pool of people. What will become of all that highly personal information? Is it properly protected?

GPS devices are making it possible to track a person's whereabouts like never before. Radio Frequency Identification devices are introducing new ways of tracking the movements of people, not just shipments to Wal-Mart.

Students and employees face some of the most discouraging privacy realities. A school official has more power to search a student in the school building than a police officer does outside of it. And most private workplaces can install all the surveillance cameras they want without violating the law.

The new health privacy laws have introduced some restrictions on how a person's health information can be used. So far, however, the laws appear to be poorly enforced.

The Internet has opened up a whole new way to track people. As websites store each user's every keystroke, they are building a massive databank of personal information. As yet, no law exists to protect all that data. Already, the federal government has tried to use that information for security purposes.

Given such evidence, it seems that people will find it increasingly difficult to guard their privacy. On the other hand, one must consider what benefits come with these privacy intrusions. On the Internet, for instance, a customer can place orders with an online company without having to enter an address and credit card number every time. Global Positioning Systems have made it possible for emergency personnel to provide faster service in response to 9-1-1 calls.

The Internet is one of many technological advances that have dramatically changed modern life and increased Americans' concerns about how to protect their privacy.

Do these benefits outweigh some loss of an individual's privacy?

Christian Parenti, in his book, *The Soft Cage: Surveillance in America from Slavery to the War on Terror*, compares the erosion of privacy to the gradual rise of Nazi power in Germany in the 1930s. He quotes essayist Milton Mayer, who described the Nazi takeover: "What happened was the gradual habituation of the people. . . . Each step was so small, so inconsequential, so well explained . . . one no more saw it developing from day to day than a farmer in his field sees the corn growing." In the end, the Nazis, through many small steps, gained complete control of the German people.

In the case of privacy, could "small steps" such as biometrics, RFID, and surveillance cameras one day add up to citizens' complete loss of privacy? Are people simply not paying enough attention?

Privacy advocates often note that young people are all too

willing to adopt new technology that threatens privacy. Teenagers post personal information on their MySpace pages, readily submit to fingerprint scans, and submit homemade videos to YouTube. They post their every thought on blogs. In fact, the adult consensus is that today's adolescents and young adults do not value privacy.

In 2006, however, Facebook, a social networking site, tried out two new features, News Feed and Mini-Feed. Facebook tracked user activity. Then, using the new features, it posted online updates about changes in members' profiles and relationships, and any new photographs. It did so without permission or instructions from its members.

Facebook members revolted. Within two days, 330,000 of them joined Students Against Facebook News Feed. Students sponsored a daylong boycott called A Day Without Facebook.

A young woman browses the social networking website Facebook. The site, started by Mark Zuckerberg, a twenty-two-year-old Harvard dropout, was the sixth most visited site in the United States in 2007.

Thousands of users signed an online petition demanding that Facebook drop the new features.

Of all the social networking sites, Facebook was known for offering users better-than-average control over their information and who could access it. Clearly, members valued these privacy options. In less than a week, Facebook executives had modified the News Feed and Mini-Feed, allowing members to disable them if they chose.

Apparently, then, young people do value privacy. They may simply draw the line of privacy at a different place than older generations.

WHOSE INFORMATION?

As the privacy debate continues to unfold, perhaps the most important question that has yet to be settled is this: "Whose data is it anyway?" Remember the stories about the Retail Credit Company and the Medical Information Bureau? Up until the 1970s, they maintained reams of personal data on millions of people. They allowed employers and businesses to access the information, but not the individuals themselves. Eventually, the public said "Enough!" New laws such as the Fair Credit Reporting Act passed in 1970 granted U.S. citizens access to these files and allowed them to correct any mistakes.

In the twenty-first century, there is a mountain of data available on almost every adult and many of the young people living in the United States. There is no comprehensive law to protect their information, however. Data brokers compile quantities of data that the old credit bureaus could only dream about. The typical data broker, such as ChoicePoint or Acxiom, draws on both public and private records to create detailed profiles on individuals. The data includes Social Security numbers, purchase records, mortgage and banking data, insurance information, and employment records. And that is just the beginning. A data broker can sort and sift this data to put together lists for marketers. For example, a data broker can provide a car dealer that sells expensive European cars the names and addresses of adults who make over $100,000 a year, have owned a European car before, and live within 100 miles (161 km) of the dealer. The car dealer can then market its cars directly to the people on the list by sending them mailings or even coupons for special deals. Brokers also provide data to businesses interested in checking the background of potential employees.

The federal government is also a major client of data brokers. In 2005 four federal agencies, including the Justice Department and the Department of Homeland Security, reportedly spent $30 million purchasing personal information from data brokers.

Data brokers deal with businesses and with the government, but usually not with individuals. According to an article in *Consumer Reports*, "When our reporters requested their own records, they were told that they could not see everything that was routinely sold to businesses. The meager information they did receive was punctuated with errors."

This brings us back to the question, "Whose data is it anyway?"

In 2006 AT&T, a major provider of telephone, wireless, and Internet services, set forth a new policy saying that it owns customer data. "While your account information may be personal to you, these records constitute business records that are owned by AT&T. As such, AT&T may disclose such records to protect its legitimate business interests, safeguard others, or respond to legal process."

This data includes calling and Internet records. AT&T says

it aggregates the data, meaning it compiles it without including users' identifications. Then it uses the data to develop in-house marketing strategies. For instance, if data show that customers place a lot of calls to Europe after seven o'clock at night, then they can develop a calling plan that takes advantage of that trend.

AT&T at least states clearly what many companies seem to assume but don't say: they own the data. When Google saves every search indefinitely, it implies that it considers that data Google's. The same is true of almost any collection of customer data maintained by a business.

When the data is violated by theft or exposed to the public as AOL did in 2006, it is not just the company that is harmed, however. Individuals are too. In which case, maybe it was the individuals' data after all.

GLOSSARY

biometric identifier: an identifier that relies on a person's physical traits, such as a fingerprint, DNA, or iris pattern in the eye. A behavioral trait, such as a person's walk, can also be used.

bioterrorism: a form of terrorism whereby terrorists deliberately release bacteria, viruses, or other germs to sicken or kill people, plants, or animals

civil liberties: a person's fundamental rights, such as freedom of speech and freedom of action, which are protected by law. In the United States, the Bill of Rights spells out civil liberties to which all citizens are entitled, free of government interference.

class action suit: a lawsuit filed on behalf of a group of people who all share the same grievance(s)

cookie: a small text file, deposited by a browser or website in a user's computer, to identify and monitor his or her online activity

dissent: in a court decision, an opinion written by the judges who hold the minority opinion (that is, the losing one)

DNA (deoxyribonucleic acid): the cellular component that carries each person's unique genetic information

encryption: the scrambling of data so that it is unreadable to unauthorized persons

forensic science: the use of science to investigate criminal cases for use in court. The use of DNA testing to identify a criminal is a form of forensic science.

GPS (Global Positioning System): a type of radio navigation system that relies on satellites to inform a user of his or her exact location

identity theft: the illegal use of an individual's personal information, such as a Social Security number and credit card number, by another person without the individual's knowledge or consent

illegal alien: a foreigner who is living in a country illegally, without proper government authority; also called "undocumented people"

RFID (radio frequency identification): an identification technology that involves three parts—a tag (also known as a transponder), a reader, and an antenna. RFID can be used to identify objects, animals, and even humans.

subpoena: a legal order commanding an individual to appear in court to testify or submit documents in a lawsuit

surveillance: keeping a close watch on someone or something

tort: a wrongdoing committed by a private citizen or group against another, for which the wronged party can file a lawsuit for damages

warrant: a written order from a judge

SOURCE NOTES

5–6   Alona Wartofsky, "Star Dreck: In SoHo, Recycling Celebrity Trash into Cash," *Washington Post*, June 21, 2004.

7   *Griswold v. Connecticut*, 381 U.S. 479 (1965).

7   Ibid.

7   *Olmstead v. United* States, 277 U.S. 483 (1928), Brandeis's dissent.

10   Ibid.

11   *Katz v. United States*, 389 U.S. 347 (1967).

12   *Kyllo v. United States*, 533 U.S. 27 (2001).

14   *California v. Greenwood*, 486 U.S. 35 (1988).

14   Stop the Drug War (DRCNet), "New Hampshire Supreme Court Says Garbage Is Protected Property," *Drug War Chronicle*, October 3, 2003, http://stopthedrugwar.org/chronicle-old/305/garbage1.shtml (April 3, 2007).

16   George Orwell, *1984*, reprinted with a foreword by Erich Fromm, (New York: Signet Classics, 1977), 1.

16   Mark Schorer, "An Indignant and Prophetic Novel," *New York Times*, June 12, 1949.

20   Louis D. Brandeis and Samuel D. Warren, "The Right to Privacy," *Harvard Law Review* 4, no. 5 (December 15, 1890): 193.

21   Amy Harmon, "Smile, You're on Candid Cell Phone Camera," *New York Times*, October 12, 2003.

21   Janet Kornblum, "Always in the Camera's Eye: Does Omnipresent Photography Put Privacy at Risk?" *USA Today*, June 27, 2006.

23   Robert Moran, "City Voters Approve Anticrime Cameras," *Philadelphia Inquirer*, May 17, 2006.

23   American Civil Liberties Union, "ACLU of Northern California Urges Fresno City Council to Reject Video Surveillance Cameras," *ACLU,* June 16, 2006, http://www.aclu.org/safefree/spying/26000prs20060616.html (April 3, 2007).

23   Ibid.

24   Tom Sowa, "Cameras Proposed for Safer Spokane: Corners, Plazas Would Be Monitored," *Spokesman Review*, June 15, 2006.

24   Paul Rogers, "Judge Says Aerial Photos of Streisand's Mansion Not Invasion of Privacy," Knight-Ridder Tribune News Service, December 4, 2003.

25   *United States v. Causby*, 328 U.S. 256 (1946).

26   Ben Dobbin, "Aerial-Imaging Becoming Indispensable," *America's Intelligence Wire*, May 8, 2006.

26   Doug Donovan, "A Bird's Eye View of Every Part of City,"

Baltimore Sun, September 7, 2004.

27 Troy Chatwin, "Spy in the Sky," Army News Service, Feb. 23, 2004.

32 Greg Toppo, "Eye Scans: A High Tech Hall Pass?" *USA Today*, February 23, 2006.

33 Ibid.

34 Ibid.

34 Fredreka Schouten, "High-Tech Screening Makes Friends, Foes in Schools," *USAToday.com*, February 4, 2004, http://www.usatoday.com/news/education/2004-02-04-biometrics-kids_x.htm (September 12, 2006).

36 Food Service Solutions, "Fingerprint Technology Quickly Gaining Ground in College Foodservice," *Food Service Solutions*, n.d., http://www.foodserve.com/FSS_Biometrics.pdf (September 15, 2006).

36 Jennifer Granholm, "Children and Minors: Privacy: Schools and School Districts: Use by School of Electronic Finger Imaging to Identify Child for School Purposes," *Office of the Attorney General (state of Michigan)*, December 12, 2000, http://www.ag.state.mi.us/opinion/datafiles/2000s/op10144.htm (September 14, 2006).

36 Claudia Graziano, "Learning to Live with Biometrics," *Wired*, September 9, 2003, http://www.wired.com/new/privacy/1,60342-0.html (September 12, 2006).

38 *New York Times*, "The Laying On of Hands for Fingerprints," June 29, 1919.

39 James D. Watson, *The Double Helix: A Personal History of the Discovery of the Structure of DNA* (New York: Signet Books, 1969), 126.

41 Council for Responsible Genetics, "Genetic Discrimination," *Council for Responsible Genetics*, 2001, http://www.gene-watch.org/programs/privacy/genetic-disc-position.html (April 3, 2007).

42 Robert Klitzman, "The Quest for Privacy Can Make Us Thieves," *New York Times*, May 9, 2006.

43 Liz Robbins, "The Knicks Have a Test Case in Medical Ethics," *New York Times*, October 15, 2005.

44 Jim Litke, "Curry at Center of 'A Fight Far Bigger than Just the Sports World,'" *USA Today,* September 28, 2005.

44 *Congressional Record*, H1237, House of Representatives, Introduction of the Genetic Information Nondiscrimination Act, March 10, 2005.

47 Richard Willing, "Officials Increase DNA profiles: Collections Made Before Convictions," *USA Today*, May 1, 2006.

49   Rick Weiss, "Vast DNA Bank Pits Policing vs. Privacy," *Washington Post*, June 3, 2005.

54   Center for Democracy and Technology, "RFID Privacy 'Best Practices' Aim to Protect Consumers," *Center for Democracy and Technology*, May 1, 2006, http://www.cdt.org/press/20060501press .php (June 28, 2006).

54   Daniel B. Wood, "Radio ID Tags Proliferate, Stirring Privacy Debate," *Christian Science Monitor*, December 15, 2004.

56   Greg Lucas, "Students Kept under Surveillance at School; Some Parents Angry over Radio Device," *San Francisco Chronicle*, February 10, 2005.

56   Ibid.

56   Electronic Privacy Information Center; *Children and RFID Systems*; anonymous parent, letter to Brittan Elementary School, January 30, 2005, June 9, 2005, http://www.epic.org/privacy/rfid/ children.html (July 10, 2006).

57   Eve Hightower, "State Bill Mirrors Sutter School's ID Fight," *Marysville (CA) Appeal-Democrat,* June 23, 2006.

57   California Senate Bill 1078, Conclusion, April 6, 2006.

59   Rob Stein, "Use of Implanted Patient Data Chip Stirs Debate on Medicine v. Privacy," *Washington Post*, March 15, 2006.

61   Annalee Newitz, "The RFID Hacking Underground," *Wired*, May 2006, http://www.wired.com/wired/archive/14.05/rfid.html (August 3, 2006).

61   Consumer Reports, "Consumer Reports Finds Personal Privacy Concerns in Planned Uses of Radio Frequency Identification Tags," *ConsumerReports.org*, May 2006, http://www.consumerreports .org/cro/cu-press-room/pressroom/archive/2006/06/eng0606tag .htm?resultPageIndex=1&resultIndex=1&searchTerm=planned %20uses%20RFIDs (April 3, 2007).

61   Bruce Schneier, "The ID Chip You Don't Want in Your Passport," *Washington Post*, September 16, 2006.

63   Mike Langberg, "Digital Footprints," *San Jose Mercury News*, June 12, 2006.

65   American Civil Liberties Union, "Profile of Rodney Goodwin," *ACLU*, December 15, 2003, http://www.aclu.org/drugpolicy/gen/ 10676re20031215.html (September 29, 2006).

66   Ibid.

68   *Tinker v. Des Moines Independent Community School District*, 393 U.S. 503 (1969).

69   *New Jersey v. T.L.O.*, 469 U.S. 325 (1985).

69   Ibid.

69   David Margolick, "Students and Privacy," *New York Times*, January 21, 1985.

70   Ibid.

71   *Vernonia School District v. Acton*, 515 U.S. 646 (1995).

71   Ibid., dissenting opinion.

72   Charles Lane, "Court to Weigh Drug Testing by Schools: Justices to Decide If Choir, Club Members' Privacy, Like Athletes', May Be Breached," *Washington Post*, March 17, 2002.

72   American Civil Liberties Union, "Justices to Hear Arguments Tomorrow in Landmark ACLU Challenge to Mandatory School Drug Testing," *ACLU,* March 18, 2002, http.//www.aclu.org/drugpolicy/testing/10665prs20020318.html (April 3, 2007).

73   Brief of *Amici Curiae*, American Academy of Pediatrics, et al., in support of respondents, *Board of Education of Pottawatomie County v. Earls*, 536 U.S. 822 (2002).

73   Ibid.

73   Brief of *Amici Curiae*, Jean Burkett et al. in support of respondents, *Board of Education of Pottawatomie County v. Earls*, 536 U.S. 822 (2002).

73   Brief of *Amici Curiae*, National School Boards Association et. al., *Board of Education of Pottawatomie County v. Earls*, 536 U.S. 822 (2002).

74   Ibid.

74   Ibid.

74   Ibid.

74   Ibid., dissenting opinion.

76   American Civil Liberties Union, "Landmark Settlement Reached in Notorious School Drug Raid Caught on Tape," *ACLU*, July 11, 2006, www.aclu.org/drugpolicy/youth/26123prs20060711.html (April 3, 2007).

77   Samuel Walker, *In Defense of American Liberties: A History of the ACLU* (New York: Oxford University Press, 1990), 308.

77   Electronic Privacy Information Center, "Student Privacy," *epic.org*, n.d., http://www.epic.org/privacy/student/ (April 3, 2007).

79   American Civil Liberties Union, "ACLU Settles Landmark Lawsuit over Release of Student Information to Military Recruiters," *ACLU*, January 27, 2006, http://www.aclu.org/privacy/youth/23962prs20060127.html (April 3, 2007).

81   Editorial, "Sacredness of Medical Records," *Hartford Courant*, June 11, 2006.

82   Associated Press, "Settlement in Privacy Suit Against Drug Store Children Allegedly Learned of Dad's AIDS from Son of Pharmacy

Clerk," *Chicago Tribune*, January 9, 1998.

84 Richard D. Lyons, "Insurance Data Called Faulty," *New York Times*, October 4, 1973.

84 Aryeh Neier, *Dossier: The Secret Files They Keep on You* (New York: Stein and Day, 1975), 141.

84 Beth Givens, "Medical Records Privacy: Fears and Expectations of Patients," *Privacy Rights Clearinghouse*, May 15, 1996, http://www.privacyrights.org/ar/speech2.htm (April 3, 2007).

86 Julie Rovner, "Hospitals, Doctors Prepare for New Medical Privacy Rules," *npr*, April 14, 2003, http://www.npr.org/templates/story/story.php?storyId=1231449 (April 3, 2007).

87 Privacy Rights Clearinghouse, "Privacy Rights Clearinghouse Files Lawsuit Charging Albertsons Violates Privacy of Pharmacy Customers by Illegally Using Their Confidential Prescription Information to Conduct Marketing Campaigns on Behalf of Drug Companies," *Privacy Rights Clearinghouse*, September 9, 2004, http://www.privacyrights.org/ar/PharmRelease.htm (June 21, 2006).

88 Kim Eagle, "Ethics: Medical Privacy vs. Healthcare Quality?" *Obesity, Fitness & Wellness Week,* July 2, 2005, 627.

88 Ibid.

88 Julie R. Ingelfinger and Jeffrey M. Drazen, "Registry Research and Medical Privacy," *New England Journal of Medicine*, April 1, 2004, 1452.

89 Eagle, "Ethics: Medical Privacy vs. Healthcare Quality?" 627.

89 *Health and Medicine Week*, "Medical Privacy Laws Frustrate Police," October 6, 2003, 303.

90 Editorial, "Sacredness of Medical Records."

91 Jared Sandberg, "Monitoring of Workers Is Boss's Right but Why Not Include Top Brass," *Wall Street Journal*, May 18, 2005.

92 Evelyn Richards, "Privacy at the Office: Is There a Right Way to Snoop," *Washington Post,* September 9, 1990.

93 American Management Association, "2005 Electronic Monitoring and Surveillance Survey: Many Companies Monitoring, Recording, Videotaping—and Firing—Employees," *American Management Association*, May 18, 2005, http://www.amanet.org/press/amanews/emsp5.htm (June 17, 2006).

94 Stephanie Armour, "More Companies Keep Track of Workers' Email," *USA Today*, June 13, 2005.

94 Jane Easter Bahls, "Mail Call," *Entrepreneur*, January 2006, 84.

94 Michael Levenson, "Video Surveillance at Work OK'd," *Boston Globe*, April 14, 2006.

95   Ibid.

95   Ibid.

96   National Workrights Institute, "Workplace Voyeurism," *National Workrights Institute*, n.d., http://www.workrights.org/issue_electronic/em_videomonitoring.html (April 3, 2007).

97   Stephanie Armour, "You Smoke? You're Fired!: Companies' Off-Duty Bans Raise a Stink," *USA Today*, May 12, 2005.

97   Ibid.

97   Jeff Angus, "Downsize What?" *CIO Insight*, September 20, 2005, http://www.cioinsight.com/article2/0,1540,1862019,00.asp (September 6, 2007).

98   *Employee Benefit News*, "Mandatory Health Screenings Reap Huge Rewards," April 1, 2006.

101   Debbie Kelley, "After 20 Years, Drug Testing Commonplace in Workplace," *Colorado Springs (CO) Gazette*, April 17, 2006.

101   Substance Abuse and Mental Health Services Administration, "Drug Testing Public Comments #8400001, Federal Register Document #04-7984," *SAMHSA*, n.d., http://www.workplace.samhsa.gov/DrugTesting/comments/PComment8400001.htm (April 3, 2007).

103   Michael Barbaro and Tom Zeller Jr., "A Face Is Exposed for AOL Searcher No. 4417749," *New York Times*, August 9, 2006.

104   Ibid.

104   Saul Hansell, "AOL Removes Search Data on Group of Web Users," *New York Times*, August 8, 2006.

104   Eric Benderoff and Jon Van, "Cameras, Cards and All Sort of Data-Gathering Techniques Can Follow Almost Your Every Move," *Chicago Tribune*, May 14, 2006.

106   *New York Times*, "Credit Data Abuses Criticized by Nader," February 8, 1971.

111   John Schwartz, "Giving Web a Memory Cost Its Users Privacy," *New York Times*, September 4, 2001.

111   Ibid.

111   Barbaro and Zeller, "A Face Is Exposed for AOL Searcher No. 4417749."

112   Hiawatha Bray, "Google Faces Order to Give up Records," *Boston Globe*, March 15, 2006.

112   *New York Times*, "Google to Keep Storing Search Requests," August 10, 2006.

112   Reece Rushing, Ari Schwartz, and Paula Bruening, "Protecting Consumers Online: Key Issues in Preventing Internet Privacy Intrusions, Fraud and Abuse," 2006, *Center for Democracy and*

Technology, http://www.cdt.org/privacy/20060724consumer.pdf (September 7, 2007).

118   John Lancaster, "House Approves Terrorism Measure: Bill Grants Bulk of Bush's Request," *Washington Post*, October 25, 2001.

118   Julia Malone, "Congress Puts Steel in Arm of Terror Law," *Atlanta Journal-Constitution*, October 26, 2001.

118   Editorial, "What is Operation TIPS?" *Washington Post*, July 14, 2002.

118   Ibid.

119   Editorial, "Ashcroft vs. Americans," *Boston Globe*, July 17, 2002.

119   Ellen Goodman, "Divided, We Spy," *Boston Globe*, July 21, 2002.

119   Butch Traylor, "Delivery Guys Won't Spy," *New York Times*, July 31, 2002.

120   Steve Kemble and Maggie Jackson, "A New and Difficult World for Frequent Fliers," *New York Times*, September 10, 2002.

121   Keith L. Alexander, "Seeing Red on Security System," *Washington Post*, March 11, 2003.

121   Ibid.

123   James Bamford, "The Agency That Could Be Big Brother," *New York Times*, December 25, 2005.

125   Bruce Schneier, "We're Giving Up Privacy and Getting Little in Return," *Minneapolis Star Tribune*, May 31, 2006.

125   Guy Gugliotta, "Data Mining Still Needs a Clue to Be Effective," *Washington Post*, June 19, 2005.

126   Lisa Graves, "NSA Pre-Recess Endgame on the Hill," *ACLU*, September 29, 2006, http://blog.aclu.org/index.php?/archives/ 70-NSA-Pre-Recess-Endgame-on-the-Hill.html (April 3, 2007).

127   Charisse Jones, "Getting a Driver's License to Get Harder," *USA Today*, March 15, 2006.

127   Ibid.

127   Pam Belluck, "Mandate for ID Meets Resistance from States," *New York Times*, May 6, 2006.

128   Ibid.

128   Knute Berger, "Real Idiocy," *Seattle Weekly*, January 18, 2006.

128   David A. Fahrenthold, "ID Law Stirs Passionate Protest in New Hampshire," *Washington Post*, May 1, 2006.

128   Judy Bohr, "Real ID Act Used to Justify Invasion of Citizens' Privacy," *America's Intelligence Wire,* March 21, 2006.

129   Belluck, "Mandate for ID Meets Resistance from States."

129   Mark Krikorian, "Loopholes in ID System Invite Terrorists, Smugglers, Illegals," *Coalition for a Secure Driver's License*, n.d.,

http://www.secure license.org/cms/index.php/plain/media__1/
news_articles/loopholes_in_id_system_invite_terrorists
_smugglers_illegals (April 3, 2007).

129 Benjamin Franklin, *Historical Review of Pennsylvania* (1759).

131   American Civil Liberties Union, "Bigger Monster, Weaker Chains:
The Growth of an American Surveillance Society," *ACLU*, January
15, 2003, http://www.aclu.org/privacy/gen/15162pub20030115.html
(April 3, 2007).

133 Christian Parenti, *The Soft Cage: Surveillance in America from
Slavery to the War on Terror* (New York: Basic Books, 2003), 208.

136 *Consumer Reports*, "Your Privacy for Sale," October 2006, 41.

136 Sara Kehaulani Goo, "Concerns Raised Over AT&T Privacy Policy,"
Washington Post, June 23, 2006.

SELECTED BIBLIOGRAPHY

Albrecht, Katherine, and Liz McIntyre. *Spychips: How Major Corporations and Government Plan to Track Your Every Move with RFID.* Nashville: Nelson Current, 2005.

Alderman, Ellen, and Caroline Kennedy. *The Right to Privacy.* New York: Vintage Books, 1997.

Bamford, James. *The Puzzle Palace: A Report on NSA, America's Most Secret Agency.* Boston: Houghton Mifflin, 1982.

Darmer, M. Katherine B., Robert M. Baird, and Stuart E. Rosenbaum, eds. *Civil Liberties vs. National Security in a Post-9/11 World.* New York: Prometheus Books, 2004.

Freedman, Russell. *In Defense of Liberty: The Story of America's Bill of Rights.* New York: Holiday House, 2003.

Halberstam, David. *The Fifties.* New York: Villard Books, 1993.

Keefe, Patrick Radden. *Chatter: Dispatches from the Secret World of Global Eavesdropping.* New York: Random House, 2005.

Neier, Aryeh. *Dossier: The Secret Files They Keep on You.* New York: Stein and Day, 1975.

Parenti, Christian. *The Soft Cage: Surveillance in America from Slavery to the War on Terror.* New York: Basic Books, 2003.

Rothfeder, Jeffrey. *Privacy for Sale.* New York: Simon & Schuster, 1992.

Walker, Samuel. *In Defense of American Liberties: A History of the ACLU.* New York: Oxford University Press, 1990.

Watson, James D. *The Double Helix: A Personal History of the Discovery of the Structure of DNA.* New York: Signet Books, 1969.

Wise, David. *The American Police State.* New York: Random House, 1976.

FURTHER READING AND WEBSITES

Books

Bridegam, Martha. *The Right to Privacy.* New York: Chelsea House, 2003.

Holtzman, David H. *Privacy Lost: How Technology Is Endangering Your Privacy.* New York: John Wiley & Sons, 2006.

Hudson, David, Jr. *Open Government: An American Tradition Faces National Security, Privacy, and Other Challenges.* New York: Chelsea House, 2005.

Lane, Frederick S. *The Naked Employee: How Technology Is Compromising Workplace Privacy.* New York: AMACOM Books, 2003.

Márquez, Herón. *George W. Bush.* Minneapolis: Twenty-First Century Books, 2007.

———. *Richard M. Nixon.* Minneapolis: Twenty-First Century Books, 2003.

O'Harrow, Robert. *No Place to Hide: Behind the Scenes of Our Emerging Surveillance Society.* New York: Free Press, 2005.

Orwell, George. *1984.* Reprinted with a foreword by Erich Fromm. New York: Signet Classics, 1977.

Rosen, Jeffrey. *The Naked Crowd: Reclaiming Security and Freedom in an Anxious Age.* New York: Random House, 2004.

Solove, Daniel J. J. *The Digital Person: Technology and Privacy in the Information Age.* New York: New York University Press, 2004.

WEBSITES

American Civil Liberties Union

http://www.aclu.org

The ACLU works to preserve and protect the rights guaranteed by the Constitution's Bill of Rights. The ACLU's national and state organizations handle numerous privacy-related cases. The ACLU's "Privacy & Technology" page offers information on a wide range of technology, surveillance, and national security issues.

Center for Democracy and Technology

http://www.cdt.org

The CDT works to improve privacy and free expression in our digital age primarily by supporting new legislation and policies. See its "Top Ten Ways to Protect Privacy Online."

Electronic Frontier Foundation

http://www.eff.org

The EFF aims to protect and promote privacy, free speech, and consumer rights in the digital world primarily through legal proceedings, such as lawsuits. Its website provides in-depth details about cases, such as its class-action suit against AT&T, and other privacy issues.

Electronic Privacy Information Center

http://www.epic.org

EPIC, which works to protect civil liberties in the digital world, maintains a comprehensive website regarding privacy and technology. Click on "Privacy A-Z" for a guide to more details on most of the issues addressed in this book, such as RFID, genetic privacy, and more. The Privacy A-Z guide also offers excellent background on federal privacy laws.

Health Privacy Project
http://www.healthprivacy.org
The Health Privacy Project website offers extensive information about health privacy and the HIPAA law. The site offers downloadable reports such as "Health Privacy: Know Your Rights."

Privacy Rights Clearinghouse
http://www.privacyrights.org
PRC is a consumer information and advocacy organization that focuses primarily on consumer privacy and technology. The site's useful fact sheets include "Privacy and the Internet: Traveling in Cyberspace Safely," "Online Shopping Tips," and "Online Job Seeker Websites: Tips to Safeguard Your Privacy."

LANDMARK FEDERAL PRIVACY LEGISLATION

1966   Freedom of Information Act (FOIA) Before the FOIA, a
        citizen's request for government records could be
        dismissed for almost any reason. Under FOIA, a citizen
        can request government records, and unless the
        requested materials fall into a legally exempt category,
        the government must provide the records.

1970   Fair Credit Reporting Act (FCRA) Before FCRA, the
        data about consumers maintained by credit bureaus
        were often incorrect and subjective, partly because
        consumers were not allowed to view their personal
        data. Under FCRA, consumers have the right to view
        their credit records and request corrections. In
        addition, the credit bureaus must follow certain
        restrictions about how they share consumer data.

1974   Privacy Act of 1974 The Privacy Act prohibits the
        sharing of government-held information about a
        citizen without the consent of the citizen, except in
        specific cases, such as for law enforcement.
        Family Educational Rights and Privacy Act (FERPA)
        Until FERPA was enacted, students and their parents had
        almost no access to their educational records, which were
        often inaccurate. Under FERPA, students and parents can
        access these records and request corrections. The school
        must obtain their consent before sharing the records with
        anyone except specially exempt organizations.

1978   Right to Financial Privacy Act This act brings Fourth
        Amendment standards to private banking records.
        Under the act, a bank can share a customer's banking
        records with the government only if the customer has

given consent or the government produces a subpoena, search warrant, or other judicially acceptable request.

1984   Cable Communications Policy Act of 1984 Under this act, cable operators may not release subscriber records without the consent of the subscriber and may not collect personally identifiable subscriber information except under certain conditions. (Internet records maintained by a cable company are not similarly protected.)   ·

1986   The Electronic Communications Privacy Act (ECPA) With this act, Congress updated existing wiretapping laws to address new forms of communications. For instance, modern wiretapping laws apply to all forms of electronic transmissions. Before the ECPA, the only legally protected communications were those transmitted by common carrier, such as a telephone call over a phone line.

1988   The Video Privacy Protection Act of 1988 Under this act, video service providers, such as video rental stores, cannot share customer rental records without the consent of the customer, except under certain conditions. The act also restricts the length of time the service provider can maintain personally identifiable customer records.

1996   Health Insurance Portability and Accountability Act of 1996 (HIPAA) HIPAA, which went into effect in 2003, restricts medical practitioners from sharing patient records with certain parties, such as employers or non-health-related businesses, without patient consent. Under HIPAA, medical practitioners can share patient records, without the patient's consent, with health-related businesses and organizations, such as insurance companies and pharmacies.

1998   Children's Online Privacy Protection Act (COPPA) of 1998 Under COPPA, a website operator must obtain parental consent before collecting personal data from a child aged twelve or younger, inform parents of the site's data collection practices, and allow parents to view and correct information on their children.

1999 **Gramm-Leach-Bliley Act (GLBA)** Under GLBA, a financial institution and its affiliates (member organizations) can share customer data with nonaffiliate institutions, unless the customer chooses to opt-out, that is, specifically request that the data not be shared. GLBA also allows states to pass stricter data-sharing laws. North Dakota financial institutions, for instance, operate under an opt-in standard, whereby a customer must give permission before the institution can share information with a nonaffiliate institution.

2001 **Uniting and Strengthening America by Providing Appropriate Tools Required to Intercept and Obstruct Terrorism Act of 2001 (USA PATRIOT Act of 2001)** This antiterrorism legislation was passed by Congress in the wake of the 9/11 attacks. It actually had a negative impact on privacy. The act greatly increases the U.S. government's ability to conduct surveillance on its citizens.

2003 **Do-Not-Call Implementation Act** This law allows the U.S. Federal Trade Commission to establish a National Do Not Call Registry. Citizens can limit the number of telemarketing calls they receive by giving their phone numbers to the registry

For a comprehensive guide to federal privacy laws, see the Center for Democracy and Technology's Guide to Online Privacy: www.cdt.org/privacy/guide/protect/laws.shtml.

LANDMARK
U.S. SUPREME COURT CASES
CONCERNING PRIVACY

1928 *Olmstead v. United States* (277 U.S. 438) The Supreme Court maintained that use of a wiretap did not violate the Fourth Amendment.

1965 *Griswold v. Connecticut* (381 U.S. 479) In this case, which challenged a Connecticut law prohibiting the use of contraceptives, the Court ruled that the right to privacy is constitutionally implied.

1967 *Katz v. United States* (389 U.S. 347) The Court determined that use of a wiretap constituted a Fourth Amendment–protected search.

1969 *Tinker v. Des Moines Independent Community School District* (393 U.S. 503) In a case involving a student's right to wear an armband to school, the Court maintained that students do not "shed their constitutional rights to freedom of speech or expression at the schoolhouse gate."

1976 *United States v. Miller* (425 U.S. 435) The Court held that bank records were not entitled to Fourth Amendment protections.

1985 *New Jersey v. T.L.O* (469 U.S. 325) The Court held that schools could meet a lower standard of "reasonable grounds" before searching a student, instead of adhering to the stricter "probable cause" standard required before conducting a search outside of the school setting.

1988 *California v. Greenwood* (486 U.S. 35) The Court upheld the right to search a person's garbage without a warrant if the garbage is set outside the home's "curtilage" (basically, the yard).

1989   *Skinner v. Railway Labor Executives' Association* (489 U.S. 602) The Court upheld the drug testing of railway employees because public safety concerns outweighed individual privacy expectations.

National Treasury Employees v. von Raab (489 U.S. 656) The Court upheld drug testing of custom agents because agents carried firearms and were involved in preventing drug trafficking. Thus, their work involved a public safety issue that outweighed individual privacy expectations.

1995   *Vernonia School District v. Acton* (515 U.S. 646) The Court upheld the schools' right to subject student athletes to random drug testing.

2001   *Kyllo v. United States* (533 U.S. 27) The Court maintained that evidence gathered by the use of a thermal imager was inadmissible because the imager could collect information that normally would be available to law enforcement officials only if they had a search warrant.

2002   *Board of Education of Pottawatomie County v. Earls* (536 U.S. 822) The Court upheld the right of schools to conduct random drug testing on students enrolled in extracurricular activities.

2004   *Hiibel v. Sixth Judicial District Court of Nevada* (542 U.S. 177) The Supreme Court ruled that statutes requiring a suspect to identify him or herself to police do not violate the Fourth or Fifth Amendments.

2006   *Hudson v. Michigan* (547 U.S. 1096) The Supreme Court held that when police fail to properly announce their arrival for the purpose of conducting a search with a warrant, any evidence they obtain during that search may still be used in court.

INDEX

aerial photography, 24–29
air travel, 120–122
Alaska Airlines, 97
Albertsons supermarket chain, 86–87
America Online (AOL), 102–104
Arnold, Thelma, 102–104
AT&T, 136–137

bar-code technology, 52
Bertillon system, 37
Bill of Rights, 7, 8
biometric physical trait identification:
    about, 31; DNA (deoxyribonucleic
    acid), 31–32, 40–49, 132;
    fingerprint identification, 34–36;
    history of, 37–40; increased use,
    15, 131–132; iris scans, 32–34
Bork, Robert, 107–108
Brandeis, Louis, 7, 19
Bureau of Investigation (BOI), 10
Bush, George W., 85, 116, 117, 118,
    122, 123–124

California v. Greenwood, 13
cameras: aerial photography, 24–26;
    cell phones, 18, 20–21; real-time
    aerial photography, 27–29;
    satellite photography, 26; video
    surveillance, 22–24
CAPPS II system, 120–122
cell phones: cameras, 18, 20–21; GPS
    technology, 63
Center for Democracy and
    Technology, 54
Children's Online Privacy Protection
    Act (COPPA), 112–113
ChoicePoint, 135
civil rights movement, 67

Coalition for a Secure Driver's
    License, 129
Cold War, 16, 39
Combined DNA Index System
    (CODIS), 46
Consolidated Freightways, 95
Constitution, U.S., 7
consumer privacy, 103–110, 113,
    135–137. See also Internet and
    computer use
Consumers Against Supermarket
    Privacy Invasion and Numbering
    (CASPIAN), 55
cookies (Internet), 110–111
credit bureaus, 105–108
Crick, Francis, 39–40
crime and criminal justice system:
    DNA evidence, 45–49; fingerprint
    evidence, 37–38; garbage
    searches, 13; and medical record
    privacy, 89; probable cause, 69;
    surveillance cameras and, 22–23;
    wiretapping, 9

data brokers, 135–136
DNA (deoxyribonucleic acid): about,
    31–32, 132; and criminal justice
    system, 45–49; discovery of,
    39–40; genetic testing and
    discrimination, 40–45
Drug-Free Workplace Act of 1988, 99
drug testing: employee, 98–101;
    student, 70–76

Electronic Privacy Information
    Center, 21
E-ZPass cards, 54–55

Fair Credit Reporting Act, 83, 84, 106
Family Educational Rights and
    Privacy Act (FERPA), 77–78
Family Locator service (Sprint), 63
Financial Services Modernization Act
    of 1999, 108–110
fingerprint identification, 34–36,
    38–39
Foreign Intelligence Surveillance Act
    (FISA), 123–124, 126
Fourteenth Amendment of the U.S.
    Constitution, 13
Fourth Amendment of the U.S.
    Constitution, 7–12

garbage, searches of, 5–6, 13–14
genetic testing and discrimination,
    40–45
global positioning systems
    technology, 62–63
Google, 111–112
Gramm-Leach-Bliley Act (GLBA),
    108–110
Griswold v. Connecticut, 7

Health Insurance Portability and
    Accountability Act of 1996, 82–83,
    85–90
Hoboken High School, 79
Homeland Security Act, 119–120
Human Genome Project, 40

identification, national system of,
    126–129
identiMetrics, 36–37
identity theft, 33
Innocence Project, 46, 48
Internet and computer use: America
    Online (AOL), 102–104; consumer
    data, 104–105; cookies, 110–111;
    employee monitoring, 91–94;
    Facebook, 134–135; Internet law,

15; legislation, 112–113; search
    engines, 102–104, 111–112
invasion of privacy law, 15
iris access system, 30, 32–34

Japanese internment, 116

Katz v. United States, 10–12
Kyllo v. United States, 12

La Crescent High School, 34–36
laws, privacy, 9–15

McCarran Act, 39
McCrackin, George, 65–67
medical records: privacy of, 40–44,
    57–60; Medical Information
    Bureau (MIB), 83–84; reform
    steps, 82–83, 85–90
medical research, 87–89
micro air vehicles (MAVs), 28
military recruitment, 78–79

Nader, Ralph, 106
national citizenship database, 128
National Security Administration
    (NSA), 122–125
*National Treasury Employees v. von
    Raab,* 99–100
New Jersey v. T.L.O., 68–69
1984 (Orwell), 16
Ninth Amendment of the U.S.
    Constitution, 13
Nixon, Richard M., 16–17, 76–77
No Child Left Behind Act, 78

Olmstead v. United States, 7, 10
Operation TIPS, 118–119
opt-in/opt-out, 108–110

Park Avenue Elementary School,
    32–34

passports, 61
personal data, 17, 113, 135–137
Philadelphia, PA, 23
Pictometry International, 25–26
privacy: data ownership, 113,
    135–137; erosion of, 131–135;
    meanings, 6–7
Privacy Act of 1974, 17
Privacy Foundation, 111
Privacy Rights Clearinghouse, 87

radio frequency identification (RFID),
    15, 52–61, 132
Reagan, Nancy, 99
Reagan, Ronald, 99
Real ID Act, 126–129
Retail Credit Company, 105–106
RFDump, 60–61
Right to Financial Privacy Act, 107,
    108

search engines, Internet, 102–104,
    111–112
Shadow 200, 27
skin implant chips, 57–61
Skinner v. Railway Labor Executives'
    Association, 99
smokers' rights, 96–97
Stratford High School, 65–67
Streisand, Barbara, 24–25
students and privacy: drug testing,
    70–76; Fourth Amendment issues,
    67–70; issues, 67; school records,
    76–78; Stratford High School raid,
    65–67

technologies, emerging, 9, 15, 21,
    113, 131–133
Teen Arrive Alive, 63
telephone wiretapping, 7, 9–12,
    122–125
thermal imaging, 12

Tinker v. Des Moines, 67–68
toll cards, electronic, 54–55
tort law, 15

United States v. Causby, 25
United States v. Miller, 107
unpiloted aerial vehicles (UAVs),
    27–29
upskirting, 21
USA PATRIOT Act, 116–118
U.S. government: National Security
    Administration (NSA), 122–125;
    overstepping legal boundaries,
    16–17; in World War II, 116. See
    also War on Terror

VeriMed microchips, 57–60
Video Privacy Protection Act of 1988,
    107–108
video surveillance, 22–24, 94–96

War on Terror: air travel, 120–122;
    Homeland Security Act, 119–120,
    Operation TIPS program,
    118–119; Real ID Act, 126–129;
    USA PATRIOT Act, 116–118
Watergate scandal, 76–77
Watson, James, 39–40
wellness programs, 97–98
Weyco, 96–97
Windber Medical Center, 93
wiretapping, 7, 9–12, 122–125
workplace privacy: educational
    records, 76; employee drug
    testing, 98–101; genetic
    discrimination, 41–45; Internet
    and computer use, 91–94; medical
    privacy, 85, 89–90; smoking,
    96–97; unhealthy habits, 96–98;
    video surveillance, 94–96
Workplace Rights Institute, 98
writ of assistance, 8–9

About the Author

Betsy Kuhn lives in Maryland with her husband and twin sons. Her books for young readers include *Angels of Mercy: The Army Nurses of World War II* and a novel, *Not Exactly Nashville*. She also wrote *Race for Space: The United States and the Soviet Union Compete for the New Frontier* for the People's History series.

Photo Acknowledgments

The images in this book are used with the permission of: © iStockphoto.com/Robert Kohlhuber, all backgrounds; © Martin Bureau/AFP/Getty Images, p. 4; National Archives, p. 8; © Arthur Schatz/Time Life Pictures/Getty Images, p. 11; © Ghislain & Marie David de Lossy/Iconica/Getty Images, p. 18; © age fotostock/SuperStock, p. 23; © Kevin Winter/Getty Images, p. 24; Photo courtesy of U.S. Army/Spc. James B. Smith Jr., p. 27; Defense Visual Information Center, p. 28; R.S. Fearing/UC Berkeley, p. 29; © William Thomas Cain/Getty Images, pp. 30, 33; AP Photo/Akron Beacon Journal, Karen Schiely, p. 35; © Hulton Archive/Getty Images, p. 37; © A. Barrington Brown/Photo Researchers, Inc., p. 40; AP Photo/Julie Jacobson, p. 43; AP Photo/Mike Derer, p. 47; © Scott Olson/Getty Images, p. 50; AP Photo/Andy Manis, p. 53; © Najlah Feanny/CORBIS, p. 55; © David Friedman/Getty Images, pp. 58, 59; AP Photo/HO, p. 62; AP Photo/Goose Creek Police Department via The Post and Courier, pp. 64, 66; © Cynthia Johnson/Time Life Pictures/Getty Images, p. 69; AP Photo/Lee Marriner, p. 72; © Robert Nickelsberg/Getty Images, p. 79; © SuperStock Inc./SuperStock, p. 80; AP Photo/Ric Francis, p. 87; © Gregor Schuster/zefa/CORBIS, p. 95; Erik Lesser/The New York Times/Redux, p. 102; © CNP/Hulton Archive/Getty Images, p. 108; © Greg Martin/SuperStock, p. 114; © Ron Sachs/CNP/CORBIS, p. 117; © Andy Nelson/The Christian Science Monitor/Getty Images, p. 120; © Jacob Silberberg/Getty Images, p. 130 (top); © iStockphoto.com/Andrew Brown, p. 130 (bottom left); © O'Donnell – CMSP/Science Faction/Getty Images, p. 130 (bottom right); © Indeed/Taxi Japan/Getty Images, p. 133; © Chris Jackson/Getty Images, p. 134. Front and back cover: © Stockbyte/Getty Images.